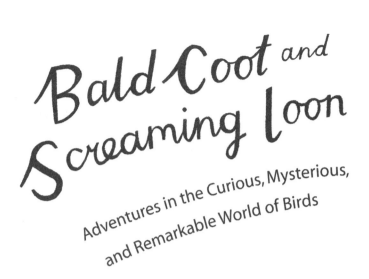

Bald Coot and Screaming Loon

Adventures in the Curious, Mysterious, and Remarkable World of Birds

Niall Edworthy

A PERIGEE BOOK

A PERIGEE BOOK
Published by the Penguin Group
Penguin Group (USA) Inc.
375 Hudson Street, New York, New York 10014, USA
Penguin Group (Canada), 90 Eglinton Avenue East, Suite 700, Toronto, Ontario M4P 2Y3, Canada
(a division of Pearson Penguin Canada Inc.)
Penguin Books Ltd., 80 Strand, London WC2R 0RL, England
Penguin Group Ireland, 25 St. Stephen's Green, Dublin 2, Ireland (a division of Penguin Books Ltd.)
Penguin Group (Australia), 250 Camberwell Road, Camberwell, Victoria 3124, Australia
(a division of Pearson Australia Group Pty. Ltd.)
Penguin Books India Pvt. Ltd., 11 Community Centre, Panchsheel Park, New Delhi—110 017, India
Penguin Group (NZ), 67 Apollo Drive, Rosedale, North Shore 0632, New Zealand
(a division of Pearson New Zealand Ltd.)
Penguin Books (South Africa) (Pty.) Ltd., 24 Sturdee Avenue, Rosebank, Johannesburg 2196, South Africa

Penguin Books Ltd., Registered Offices: 80 Strand, London WC2R 0RL, England

While the author has made every effort to provide accurate telephone numbers and Internet addresses at the time of publication, neither the publisher nor the author assumes any responsibility for errors, or for changes that occur after publication. Further, the publisher does not have any control over and does not assume any responsibility for author or third-party websites or their content.

BALD COOT AND SCREAMING LOON

First American edition: March 2010
Originally published in Great Britain in 2009 by Transworld Publishers.

Perigee hardcover ISBN: 978-0-399-53568-0

PRINTED IN THE UNITED STATES OF AMERICA

10   9   8   7   6   5   4   3   2   1

Most Perigee books are available at special quantity discounts for bulk purchases for sales promotions, premiums, fund-raising, or educational use. Special books, or book excerpts, can also be created to fit specific needs. For details, write: Special Markets, Penguin Group (USA) Inc., 375 Hudson Street, New York, New York 10014.

To my godchildren,
Hope Farquhar
and
Charlie Barnett

Among those [bird lovers] I know of are a Prime Minister, a President, three Secretaries of State, a charwoman, two policemen, two Kings, two Royal Dukes, one Prince, one Princess, a Communist, seven Labour, one Liberal, six Conservative Members of Parliament, several farm-labourers earning ninety shillings a week, a rich man who earns two or three times more than that every hour of the day, at least forty-six schoolmasters, an engine-driver, a postman, and an upholsterer.

**BRITISH ORNITHOLOGIST, NATURALIST, BROADCASTER AND AUTHOR
JAMES FISHER (1912–70)**

I hope you love birds, too. It is economical. It saves going to Heaven.

EMILY DICKINSON (1830–86)

CONTENTS

INTRODUCTION

AS A YOUNG TEENAGER in the late seventies I spent an entire spring vacation living in the shrubbery of my garden, painstakingly capturing images of dozens of different species of birds. Using my dad's 1959-vintage Kodak Reflex S with 135mm telephoto lens, for two and a half weeks I snapped shots of all manner of finches, tits and other commonplace garden birds, and occasionally slightly more exotic visitors such as nuthatches, tree creepers, a couple of blackcaps and a green woodpecker, which was a rare sight even then.

Day after day I tiptoed and crawled among roses, camellias and lilac, caked in mud and streaked with thorn scratches, in search of the perfect image. I saw myself as a cross between Ansel Adams and

David Attenborough, a martyr to the twin causes of art and natural history. I had found not one hobby but two, and it was exciting to be able to combine them in one major project.

At the end of the first week, I carefully opened the camera to remove the 72 precious exposures . . . and saw that I had forgotten to put in a roll of film.

No problem, these things happen, I thought – even to professionals. The captain of the *Titanic*, after all, was no amateur. I went back to the undergrowth to continue my communion with nature and set about capturing a series of even more stunning images than the ones that, sadly, had been lost to future generations of art and nature lovers.

For a further week or so I worked the shrubbery – the trampled tulips sacrificed for the wider cause – searching for the perfect angle from which to secure sometimes thoughtful, sometimes playful but always exquisite images of blue tit families on peanut feeders, thrushes pulling worms from the moist, warming soil and cocky robins sitting on the fence waiting to peck out the eyes of their neighborhood rivals.

This time there were no silly technical errors regarding the installation of the film roll and, just to be on the safe side, I took the package of film to the mailbox myself and sent it off to Happy Snaps, or whatever they were called, to be developed.

A few days later, the postman handed me a large colorful envelope containing my 72 brilliant prints . . . Only there didn't appear to be any. I turned the envelope upside down and shook out its contents. Leaflets, brochures and pre-paid envelopes tumbled onto the doormat, but no photos. The imbecile envelope-licker at Crappy Snaps had failed to lick the envelope properly and the photos must have fallen out en route! (He was probably too busy licking the windows in his office.)

In that one moment of awful disappointment, my interest in birds and photography vanished.

By the end of the day, I had returned to what teenagers did best back then, namely beating up my brother, admiring soccer star Kevin Keegan and watching *It's a Knockout*. Birds were just stupid. They could keep their fancy colorful plumage, extraordinary flying capabilities and magical migration skills – the sad, ironic truth was that they didn't have brains big enough to realize that they were just, to quote my disillusioned teenage self, "peanut-eating arseholes," one up the food chain from the insects.

If all 10,000 of the world's bird species had become extinct over the following 20 years, I can honestly say I don't think I would have noticed. I buried birds deep down in my consciousness, imagining, so help me God, that they would never take wing in my life again. I don't have a single memory of an encounter with a bird during that time. They were just there, flapping and fretting about in the background, no more or less interesting to me than the trees in which they perched or the skies in which they flew.

As for the people who wasted their lives watching and recording the silly creatures, well, they were just plain weird. A twitcher was just a trainspotter in slightly superior rainwear and like his cousin, the flasher, he sported Dark Age quantities of facial hair and spent an unhealthy amount of time skulking around in the undergrowth of large municipal parks, beauty spots and coastal paths. He was an "enthusiast" and, as such, a crashing bore to be avoided at all costs. I have since discovered that the term "twitcher" is used disparagingly by the true nature lovers within the birding community to describe the highly competitive box-ticker – a sub-species of the trainspotter – who drops whatever he's doing and drives very fast to the other end of the country upon news that a Kentish plover has been spotted in a puddle somewhere. To the twitcher, a rare bird is not a creature of uncommon beauty and curiosity but a name and number to be logged and shown off to rivals.

Quite how I came to rediscover a love and fascination for birds is more difficult to explain than how I went into denial about them as a spotty teenager almost a quarter of a century earlier. There has been no single trigger, no heart-stopping encounter with a golden eagle, no sighting of an exotic hoopoe or bee-eater in my back garden, just a gradual reawakening to the magical enigma of these remarkable creatures.

A major factor was certainly moving from the city to the countryside. The garden of our city home comprised 16 patio slabs, three high bare walls and a plastic sandpit. Ants and rats were the only wildlife in residence. The garden of our new home, though not large, is filled with trees, shrubs and plants and backs onto a large field that stretches north up the slopes of the South Downs. The wildlife abounds. I see it and hear it all day long. It is a special kind of fool that moves to a new world and fails to be curious about his surroundings; it's been impossible not to take an interest in the creatures with which I share my plot of land. Thus mild curiosity turned to passing interest; passing interest swelled into mounting fascination and mounting fascination ballooned into a child-like enthrallment bordering on obsession. Next stop, divorce and the madhouse.

Today, our garden is full of feeders, bird tables and baths; I have two pairs of binoculars – one upstairs and one downstairs – and more than 100 books on birds, including a handful of pocket guides which I leave on windowsills for quick identification. I squint into hedgerows and stand motionless in fields and woods like a man who has forgotten what it is he is meant to be doing. My friends are baffled. My wife looks on sympathetically, wondering what on earth has happened to me.

For me, it's not so much the great beauty and variety of birds – although that is undoubtedly some of the attraction – nor is it that these creatures can fly, although that too will always be part of the magic. Nor is it that twice a year, every year, billions of them migrate thousands of miles, using the stars and the sun, the earth's magnetic field and changes in the weather to guide them to exactly the place to which they and their forebears have been travelling since prehistory – although that too will for ever remain one of nature's great dramas and mysteries.

Many bird species are under grave threat of extinction in the coming decades and the urge to help them survive is a powerful one, but again that is only part of the appeal. So too is the knowledge that there are dozens of species out there, most of them in what remains of our rain forests, that have yet to be discovered.

As we live in the so-called Information Age, the impression has been put about that there is little today that human understanding has not yet grasped. Yes, there are hundreds of problems facing civilization and the environment, but it's a lack of will and resources that prevents us from solving them. Ignorance isn't the issue. Birds, however, continue to be something of a mystery and this inscrutability certainly explains some of their charm. Birds don't give up their secrets easily. Wild birds are difficult to study as their natural behavior cannot be observed in captivity. To understand a bird, you have to study it in its wild home and – as they are flighty creatures – that can be difficult.

Until I began to read up on the subject, it was my understanding that the eggheads had cracked all the riddles of the natural sciences, including the strange habits of birds that had so intrigued our ancestors over the centuries and had fired the imagination of so many of our poets, musicians and artists. The mystique of these creatures, I'd thought, had been laid bare by scientific research. Not so, it turns out. It has been a thrill to discover that there is plenty about birds that scientists still cannot explain and plenty more of which they are only half certain. It's exciting that there are still many things about our world we don't understand, that not everything has yet been conquered by human progress and scientific endeavor. There are still outposts resisting the advance of knowledge.

Unlike most other animals, birds play out their lives right before our very eyes, from birth to death. This year I have watched a pair of collared doves raising their chicks in an alarmingly scruffy and unstable-looking nest in the little satellite dish screwed onto the eastern wall of the house. I have watched sparrows and finches mobbing a piratical magpie in a frenzy of flapping and screeching and, when they appeared to be losing the Battle of the Bird Table, the two doves swooped down from their nest and drove off the invader.

I have seen the breathtaking spectacle of a pair of red kite, a species recovering from the brink of extinction in Britain, soaring above the field behind. A little egret, another rare species making a comeback, lives by the small river a few hundred yards from the front door. Kingfishers live or visit there too and every now and then I catch sight of one of these shy, jumpy creatures as it darts for cover in a blur of turquoise and orange.

Death stalks a bird throughout its life. Only a modest fraction of our common garden birds survive into a second year, most of them falling prey to starvation, injury, disease or predation. In one spring day, I saw a young wood pigeon taken by a sparrowhawk and an over-confident robin snatched from mid-air by a cat. And yet the effort they put into their lives, the urgency to live, is astonishing and uplifting. Just watch blue tits making hundreds of trips in a single day to and from the flower beds to build their nests for the breeding season.

In the late winter and spring, I am woken every morning by the insane chatter of the dawn chorus, with so many songs and calls filling the air that if I close my eyes it's easy to imagine that I have woken up under the rain-forest canopy. These are the sounds of love and war as the males burst with song to attract the females and see off their rivals for the territory.

Two or three years ago, I would have seen but not noticed, heard but not listened to any of these remarkable performances of nature. They are not put on for our enjoyment, but they are there if we want them.

If you take an interest in birds, then you must take an interest in their habitat – the world in which they live – and if you do that then you have assumed a curiosity and concern about the wider environment. To be interested in the environment is to be interested in our own habitat, and once that starts to hold your attention you have become interested in the future. You have become interested in life itself. Birds, for me, have confirmed that ours is a life worth living.

Dinosaurs in Disguise?

HOW BIRDS CAME TO BE

Are birds really descended from dinosaurs?

The answer is somewhere between very probably and almost certainly, yet there is still some debate because the evidence about how and when birds evolved is not conclusive. To some ornithologists, on the other hand, the mystery is not whether birds are descended from dinosaurs but whether they *are* dinosaurs.

The bird–dinosaur debate began with the discovery in 1860 of a fossil in a limestone quarry in Bavaria that astounded the scientific community of the day. The 145-million-year-old fossil is a crow-sized skeleton covered in feathers and it has been so well preserved that even from a picture you can see that the creature was part bird, part reptile. It was dubbed "Archaeopteryx," meaning ancient wing, and it is considered to be one of the most important fossil finds ever. The feathers, which are unique to birds, are obvious but the skeleton is very unbird-like with its long bony tail, teeth in place of a beak and claws on the wings, giving it a strong resemblance to the running lizard dinosaurs. If there had been no feathers with Archaeopteryx, it would have been wrongly classified as a small dinosaur, just as five previous finds had been. One was displayed in a museum as a running lizard dinosaur for decades before it was realized it was in fact Archaeopteryx.

The majority of ornithologists contending that birds are descended from dinosaurs point out that the two classes of creature share almost 100 physical characteristics, which is far more evidence than they would need to prove their case in a court of law. And in the last 15 years or so, archaeologists have unearthed even more evidence,

~~~~~~~~

I once had a sparrow alight upon my shoulder for a moment, while I was hoeing in a village garden, and I felt that I was more distinguished by that circumstance than I should have been by any epaulet I could have worn.

NATURALIST AND WRITER
HENRY DAVID THOREAU
(1817–62)

~~~~~~~~

including dinosaurs with bird-like features and primitive birds with dinosaur-like features.

The evidence, in both living birds and fossils, to support the theory that birds have evolved from two-legged, running dinosaurs is highly convincing, but it doesn't quite clinch the argument. There are still gaps in the fossil record and other small pockets of doubt that the skeptics, like woodpeckers to a tree trunk, cling on to for the time being – if for no other reason than the sake of a good scientific quarrel. They believe that birds evolved from four-legged reptiles that lived in trees, insisting that any similarity between birds and dinosaurs is an example of convergent evolution, whereby two distinct, unrelated groups of creature coincidentally grow to resemble each other because they happen to live in similar environments.

Why not fur or scales like the rest of us?

Among the many characteristics that birds share with their putative dinosaur ancestors and with present-day reptiles, one of the most telling about their genetic relationship is a protein called keratin. The scaly skin of a reptile and the feathers of a bird are both composed of this robust fibrous compound, which strongly suggests that the latter evolved from the former. What's more, birds still have scales on the lower parts of their legs and feet. The theory is that dinosaurs (or other reptiles) with frayed scales may have had a genetic advantage because they were able to trap air and thus keep warmer than the reptiles with standard scales, which had to wait for the sun to climb high into the sky to warm themselves by lying in its rays. The frayed scales, which slowly grew in length into feathers, helped conserve their owners' energy, enabling the creatures to get to food sources first in the early morning. The sunbathers, meanwhile, will have been weaker in the morning and more sluggish in the ensuing scrap for food. Some of these latter species probably died out while their frayed and feathered cousins moved onwards and upwards.

> Taking Archaeopteryx as the first bird, scientists estimate that a minimum of 150,000 to 175,000 different species of birds have existed throughout history, though some put the figure as high as 1.5 million. There are approximately 10,000 species alive today.

There are other advantages to plumage that will have added even greater selective pressure: feathers gave birds camouflage and features to display during courtship, and above all the ability to fly.

Taking the evolutionary express

Scientists are constantly amazed by the speed at which birds have mutated into a new form to suit an environment. Incontrovertible proof of this can be seen on the Galapagos Islands, which emerged from the Pacific Ocean floor to the west of Ecuador following a volcanic eruption roughly five million years ago (a short time in evolutionary terms). Birds began to arrive not long afterwards and, without any predators there to worry about, they quickly settled into a cozy existence, gorging on the abundant fish to be found around the islands and doing what they're programmed to do, namely reproducing to continue their genetic line, as efficiently and actively as possible. The islands' cormorants no longer needed wings and over time they grew shorter and shorter as the creatures evolved into the flightless birds we see there today.

The Archaeopteryx's Song

I am only half out of this rock of scales.
What good is armour when you want to fly?
My tail is like a stony pedestal
and not a rudder. If I sit back on it
I sniff winds, clouds, rains, fogs where
I'd be, where I'd be flying, be flying high.
Dinosaurs are spicks and
all I see when I look back
is tardy turdy bonehead swamps
whose scruples are dumb tons.
Damnable plates and plaques
Can't even keep out ticks.
They think when they make the ground thunder
as they lumber for a horn-lock or a rut
that someone is afraid, that everyone is afraid,
but no one is afraid. The lords of creation
are in my mate's next egg's next egg's next egg,
stegosaur. It's feathers I need, more feathers
for the life to come. And these iron teeth
I want away, and a smooth beak
to cut the air. And these claws
on my wings, what use are they
except to drag me down, do you imagine
I am ever going to crawl again?
When I first left that crag
and flapped low and heavy over the ravine
I saw past present and future
like a dying tyrannosaur
and skimmed it with a hiss.

I will teach my sons and daughters to live
on mist and fire and fly to the stars.

SCOTTISH POET EDWIN MORGAN (1920–)

Evolution just a breeze

To many people, the feral pigeon, a familiar sight waddling along the pavements and squares of our cities and towns, is an ugly, un-hygienic bird, a "rat with wings" that should be shunned or even exterminated. But even its many detractors would have to acknowledge that the bird is one of the most successful species on the planet, with a rare ability to adapt with great speed to new environments and thereby ensure its survival – indeed increase. Such is its adaptability that the only place in the world where you won't find the feral pigeon is on the polar ice-caps. It has colonized everywhere else, which is no mean achievement for a species whose natural habitat was a rocky coastline until man began to domesticate the bird about the time of William the Conqueror. Since then, the birds have slowly moved into our towns where the food is plentiful and where the buildings provide similar, but much warmer homes than wind-blasted cliffs. No relation of the wood pigeon that nests in trees, the "feral" descended from the rock dove, but it is now extremely rare to find them living on coastlines. Most creatures take hundreds of thousands, even millions of years to leave one environment and adapt to another, but the unfancied feral pigeon has done it in under a millennium. So next time you walk past a "feral" as it plucks some cold French fries out of a trash can, raise your hat and give it a nod of respect.

The raven and the dove are the first birds to be mentioned by name in the Bible:

> Then it came about at the end of forty days, that Noah opened the window of the ark which he had made; And he sent out a raven, and it flew here and there until the water was dried up from the earth. Then he sent out a dove from him, to see if the water was abated from the face of the land; But the dove found no resting place for the sole of her foot, so she returned to him into the ark, for the water was on the surface of all the earth. Then he put out his hand and took her, and brought her into the ark to himself. So he waited yet another seven days; and again he sent out the dove from the ark. The dove came to him toward evening, and behold, in her beak was a freshly picked olive leaf. So Noah knew that the water was abated from the earth. Then he waited yet another seven days, and sent out the dove; but she did not return to him again.
>
> **Genesis 8:6–12**

~~~~~~~~~~~~~~~~~~~~~~~~~~~~~~~

I value my garden more for being full of
blackbirds than cherries, and very frankly
give them fruit for their songs.
ENGLISH ESSAYIST JOSEPH ADDISON (1672–1719)

~~~~~~~~~~~~~~~~~~~~~~~~~~~~~~~

❝ A turkey is more occult and awful than all the angels and archangels. In so far as God has partly revealed to us an angelic world, he has partly told us what an angel means. But God has never told us what a turkey means. And if you go and stare at a live turkey for an hour or two, you will find by the end of it that the enigma has rather increased than diminished. **❞**

ENGLISH WRITER G. K. CHESTERTON (1874–1936)

Beastly business

Bestiaries, popular in Europe in the Middle Ages, were books containing elaborate illustrations, descriptions of animals and often moral lessons to be drawn from their behavior. Below are extracts from a bestiary from http://bestiary.ca:

THE PARROT IS A BIRD *found in India that can be taught to speak like a man. It learns better when it is young, but if it will not learn one must hit it over the head with an iron bar. It can say "ave" by nature, but must be taught all other words. Its beak is so hard that if the parrot falls from a height it can break its fall with its beak. Parrots are coloured green with a purple-red collar; they hate the rain because the water makes their colours appear ugly. There are two kinds of parrot: the kind with three toes have a mean disposition, but the ones with six toes are gentle.*

THE OWL HAUNTS RUINS *and flies only at night; preferring to live in darkness it hides from the light. It is a dirty, slothful bird that pollutes its own nest with its dung. It is often found near tombs and lives in caves. Some say it flies backward. When other birds see it hiding during the day, they noisily attack it to betray its hiding place. Owls cry out when they sense that someone is about to die.*

THE NIGHTINGALE HAS A SWEET SONG*, and loves to sing. It sings to relieve the tedium as it sits on its nest through the night. At dawn it sings so enthusiastically that it almost dies. Sometimes nightingales compete with each other with their songs, and the one that loses the competition often dies.*

THE HOOPOE *is said to be a filthy bird that collects human dung and builds its nest with it, and eats bad-smelling excrement. It also likes to live around tombs. It is further said* *that if the blood of the hoopoe is rubbed on a sleeping man, devils will try to strangle him.*

AT NIGHT, CRANES
take turns keeping watch for enemies. The one who is on duty holds a stone up with one claw; if the watcher falls asleep the stone will fall and wake him. If the wind is strong cranes swallow sand or carry stones for ballast. Cranes are the enemy of pygmies, with whom they are constantly at war.

THE FLESH OF THE PEACOCK *is so hard that it does not rot, and can hardly be cooked in fire or digested by the liver. Its voice is terrible, causing fear in the listener when the bird unexpectedly begins to cry out. Its head is like a snake, its breast is sapphire-coloured, it has red feathers in its wings, and has a long green tail adorned with eyes. If it receives praise for its beauty, it raises its tail, leaving its rear parts bare. When it suddenly awakes it cries out, because it thinks its beauty has been lost. It is a bird with great foresight. Its feet are very ugly, so the peacock refuses to fly high in order to keep its feet hidden.*

AS YOUNG PELICANS GROW, *they begin to strike their parents in the face with their beaks. Though the pelican has great love for its young, it strikes back and kills them. After three days, the mother pierces her side or her breast and lets her blood fall on the dead birds, and thus revives them. Some say it is the male pelican that kills the young and revives them with his blood.*

A rare old bird indeed

The kiwi is a mighty queer creature, a fine example of how evolution will quickly dump some characteristics and replace them with others if left undisturbed for a few million years. Once upon a time, the ancestors of this endangered nocturnal bird could fly perfectly well, but today it has more in common with a hedgehog than with its feathered cousins. Found only in New Zealand, where it is strictly protected by law, this friendly, chicken-sized bird has wings that have been reduced by lack of use to no more than 2 inch feathered stumps. In a land with no mammals to prey on it – until man arrived – the kiwi, like its flightless cousins the ostrich and the emu, had no reason to fly. Spending so much time on the ground, it developed an incredible sense of smell, using its long, slender, flexible bill, which has nostrils at the lower end, to forage for insects, grubs and worms on the forest floor – just as a pig or a hedgehog does.

Unlike its moa cousins and countless other species of New Zealand birds, the kiwi managed to survive the twin onslaught of man and his land mammals for two main reasons. First, it is highly alert to possible danger and although it may look ungainly it can outrun a human being. Then, if it does fail to escape its predator, it can deliver a flesh-tearing blow with its sharp, three-toed feet that will make even the hungriest or most determined interloper think twice about having a second go.

Number of different species	
Amphibians	6,000
Reptiles	8,000
Birds	10,000
Fish	30,000
Insects	Countless millions

Why the ostrich gave up flying

All animals are programmed to expend as little energy as possible, so if a local ecology presents a bird with the chance of giving up on the exhausting business of flight it will take it with open wings. All flightless birds such as the kiwi, emu, rhea and cassowary retain all the major physical features to indicate that their ancestors once flew the skies, but over time, exploiting the favorable conditions on the ground, they adapted to a life on their feet, sprouting long powerful legs to make up for their inability to escape from predators by taking to the air. At full pelt, an ostrich can reach speeds of 50 mph and they could outrun most athletes for more than 20 minutes.

The ostrich is the tallest and heaviest bird in the world and its flightless cousins, with the exception of the kiwi, are huge too, but if they could still fly, they would be a fraction of their gargantuan size. The ostrich is to the wren what an elephant is to a pygmy mouse and its scale is key to its evolutionary success because it serves as a deterrent in itself. The ostrich weighs between eight and 12 times more than the kori bustard, the world's heaviest flying bird. You'd have to be insensible with drink or stark raving mad to fight an ostrich, but if the whim ever took you, be warned that with one kick your feathered opponent could crush your skull, break your spine or rip out your innards.

❝ Let us, before leaving the subject, once more look back across that awesome gulf of 150 million years to the days when Archaeopteryxes hopped about on the shores of the reedy pools in Bavaria. It is hard to conceive so long a time. The mind does not comprehend it. Imagine a line 150 feet long, each foot representing a million years; ourselves a point at this end, Archaeopteryx a point at the other. If we start moving toward the ancient bird, we shall find that by the time we have passed the days of Tut-ankh-amen's great-grandfather, we shall have progressed a distance about equal to the width of a thick pencil-line, or one millimetre to 3333 years. After going back the vast space of a third of an inch we shall have passed far beyond historic times to the early Stone Age of Man, and at the end of an inch we shall be well into Glacial times. The first foot of our 150-foot journey will have brought us only to the beginning of the latest or Pleistocene epoch of earth's history, and we will have accomplished less than half the journey ere we reach the fauna of the Paris basin and the great Diatryma of Eocene days. And even when we at length reach the journey's end, we are still a long way from the starting point of birds. Thus we may realize that geologically speaking a thousand years is not really such a very long time; it is only that our thoughts are small. ❞

GLOVER MORRILL ALLEN (1879–1942), *BIRDS AND THEIR ATTRIBUTES*

The Cloaca Monologues

COURTSHIP AND BREEDING

Why do some birds settle down with partners and others play the field?

It is often said that 90 percent of birds are monogamous, but recent studies have exploded this myth. A small percentage of birds, generally the larger ones that live longer, such as the swan and the albatross and most birds of prey, do settle down for life. But most animals aren't built to stay faithful to one partner. On the contrary, they are "hardwired" to put it about as much as possible: the male to spread his genes far and wide, and the female to choose the fittest mate to father and help rear the chicks. Monogamy is a risk that most animals, including birds, cannot afford to take.

Scientists now in fact draw a distinction between sexual monogamy (mating exclusively with one partner during the breeding season) and social monogamy (pairing up with a mate to raise offspring but also having a bit on the side if the opportunity presents). In one famous study, female blackbirds that paired with sterilized males still laid eggs that hatched. So while most birds, including all those in your back garden, like to pop to the hedge next door "to borrow some berries," 90 percent of birds are *socially* monogamous. This form of monogamy works for both sexes. The female gets an extra pair of mandibles to help around the home, building the nest, foraging for food, feeding chicks, disposing of waste, maybe even keeping the eggs warm. The male, meanwhile, gets to fulfill his main purpose in life, namely to continue the family line.

The Birds

He. Where thou dwellest, in what grove,
    Tell me Fair One, tell me Love;
    Where thou thy charming nest dost build,
    O thou pride of every field!

She. Yonder stands a lonely tree,
    There I live and mourn for thee;
    Morning drinks my silent tear,
    And evening winds my sorrow bear.

He. O thou summer's harmony,
    I have liv'd and mourn'd for thee;
    Each day I mourn along the wood,
    And night hath heard my sorrows loud.

She. Dost thou truly long for me?
    And am I thus sweet to thee?
    Sorrow now is at an end,
    O my Lover and my Friend!

He. Come, on wings of joy we'll fly
    To where my bower hangs on high;
    Come, and make thy calm retreat
    Among green leaves and blossoms sweet.

ENGLISH POET WILLIAM BLAKE (1757–1827)

How do birds have sex?

This is not a straightforward business: bird breeding is like speed-dating with fighting; like sailors of old enjoying a run ashore after months at sea, only noisier and tougher. For most species, it goes something like this: the male starts staking out his territory in mid-winter, beats up or sees off any rivals that dare enter his patch, puts on his finest plumage (see peacocks) and/or starts to sing as loudly and attractively as he can to alert passing females, and then fixes a date with a mate – or several if he's playing the field.

The male really has his work cut out trying to woo the female, because she tends to reject his first few approaches, forcing him to try a bit harder each time until he's almost worn himself out. She needs him to prove his fitness to father her young. Males sometimes have to fight off rivals for their mate's affection and once he succeeds in winning over the female, the next stage of the relationship is to build a nest. For most birds this is a joint enterprise.

Then, and only then, does the new couple finally get down to copulating – and this part is a very quick affair, surprising perhaps after all that scrapping and prancing about. Blink and you'll miss it. After a bit of awkward fumbling and maneuvering, the male mounts the female in a flash. Sperm is passed over when the male's cloaca, a hole under his tail also used for excreting, is conjoined with the female's. This is known as a "cloacal kiss." The female turns the fertilized ovum into a newly laid egg in just 24 hours. As the female, typically, stores the sperm for days or even weeks, copulation need take place only once, though it may occur several times.

Birds of prey, and large waders and shorebirds, will probably produce two eggs, laid two or three days apart; most other birds lay an egg every day, the overall number varying greatly between species.

The pair then incubate their clutch for however long it takes (in the case of most songbirds, roughly two to three weeks). Once the chicks hatch, the parents feed them until they are ready to fledge, making hundreds of trips each day to and from the nest to deliver food. Some species have been recorded making more than 1,000 trips a day. If you have ever wondered why the birds in your backyard look a little tattered and disheveled toward the end of the summer, now you know. Their offspring have literally run them ragged. Once the breeding season is over, the bird's reproductive organs shrivel up to reduce its weight for flying. The death rate among common backyard birds is very high; they are doing well if they survive in their first year of life to experience a single breeding season of their own. In temperate regions, the peak breeding season is roughly March to June, when food sources for the young, such as caterpillars and flying insects, are most abundant.

Mute swans are one of just a handful of bird species that take a partner for life. The "divorce rate" among mute swan couples is roughly 5 percent. (The equivalent figure for the Bewick's swan, a Siberian bird that winters in Britain, is even lower, at less than 1 percent.) Mutes don't rush into their relationships either; courtship is elaborate and flirtatious, resuming at the start of each breeding season. The courting couple indulge in a theatrical display of affection known as "head-turning," in which the two birds touch breasts and, inadvertently of course, form the shape of a heart. The male, or cob, is highly protective of his partner, the nest the pair build and the young they produce and it's best to give cobs a wide berth during the breeding season. Swans' parenting behavior is similar to the traditional human model, with the male as the protector and the female as the nurturer, although the male will "help around the house" too. Both will look after the cygnets and take them for rides on their backs to keep them safe from predators.

> **Serial adulterers**
> Over 50 percent of reed bunting chicks are not fathered by the pair male but are the result of an adulterous liaison, the highest recorded rate of "infidelity" among any bird species.

How birds manage to build nests, often highly elaborate ones, is one of nature's greatest miracles. Try making one with your hands using twigs, hair, spittle and moss, and see how far you get. Now try making one with your mouth. The fact that birds can make them using just a beak, often to minute specifications and incredibly intricate designs, is remarkable. Some nests are conspicuously scruffy, such as those of doves, pigeons, house sparrows and crows, but most are elaborate structures built to design specifications unique to their species. Constructing the future family home takes a huge amount of effort and expenditure of energy. Long-tailed tits, for instance, use roughly 2,000 feathers in building a nest and fly over 600 miles to collect all the materials. Spiders are vital to birds in the breeding season as their sticky webs are used by a great number of birds as a glue or mortar for binding together the main construction materials of twigs, moss, grasses, hair and feathers.

~~~~~~~~~~~~~~~~~~~~~~~~~~~~~~~~~~~

And I beheld the birds in the bushes building their nests, which no man, with all his wits, could ever make. And I marvelled to know who taught the magpie to lay the sticks in which to lay her eggs and to breed her young; for no craftsman could make such a nest hold together, and it would be a wonderful mason who could construct a mould for it.

WILLIAM LANGLAND (C. 1330–86), *PIERS PLOWMAN*

~~~~~~~~~~~~~~~~~~~~~~~~~~~~~~~~~~~

The penthouse mansion of the bald eagle

Bald eagles build enormous nests, measuring up to 10 feet across and weighing as much as two tons, the equivalent off a fully loaded 4 × 4 off-road vehicle. Eagles mate for life and often use the same nest year after year, adding more and more sticks at the start of each breeding season. The nests are usually built in large trees with a commanding view of the area close to rivers or coastline so that the giant predators are able to capture fish for their chicks without having to travel too far away and leave them unattended. Sometimes the nests will crash to the ground under their own weight and the pair will have to quickly build a makeshift home or wait. Living to the age of 30, there is no great urgency for a bald eagle to produce a chick, and some pairs will take a year off if the weather conditions aren't right or if there's a shortage of food. The female lays between one and three eggs, but usually two, and if food is in short supply the older, bigger chick will kill its sibling without any protest from the parents.

Bald eagles will also nest on cliffs or even on the ground in areas of Alaska and northern Canada where there is a shortage of suitable-sized trees, but they are quick to abandon a nest if they are disturbed. Eagles use old sticks from the ground, but sometimes break branches off trees with their beaks and talons. After weaving the sticks together, they line the nest with softer materials, including long grasses, mosses, cornstalks and their own feathers. Scientists are yet to crack the mystery of why, during incubation, the male bald eagle brings back fresh sprigs of conifer branches. Theories that have been suggested include use as an insect repellent, deodorant or shade.

The lengths males will go to . . .

Male birds often have to go the extra mile – and more – to attract a mate. Songbirds sing until they almost burst with the effort; the male wren builds over a dozen nests for the female to choose from; the tern brings a fish as a love gift; cranes dance together; the peregrine falcon, the world's fastest creature, stages a spectacular aerobatic display; swans go on a protracted date before committing, and the male peacock has – over tens of millions of years – developed the most spectacular fan of tail feathers for the sole purpose of attracting a female. But the grebe conducts the most elaborate and romantic courtship ritual (at least to sentimental, dewy-eyed humans), with male and female meeting breast to breast and then dancing with each other for several days.

Pluck off, pal, she's mine

Contrary to popular belief, it is not the striking colorful plumage of the cock pheasant that sets hens' hearts a-flutter in the breeding season, it's the red, fleshy lobes – or "wattles" – hanging off his face. When the male is aroused, the wattles inflate, their size telling the female everything she needs to know about his physical well-being, including testosterone levels. Pheasant breeding is a supreme form of selective breeding, regulated not by man but by their own instinctive behavior, an avian Nazi-style eugenics program happening right here, on the other side of our hedges. The fittest males attract the most females – which explains why you often see half a dozen of the dull, brown females following one brightly colored male. They frequently end up all living together in a kind of polygamy. Top males pull all the birds and get to fulfill their raison d'être, to continue their line, leaving the losers to hop about in the undergrowth and wait to get shot by a chinless man in knickers high on sherry and brandy. The "loser" birds often hang around other pheasants in the hope of jumping an unsuspecting female when the big, scary stud pheasant with massive wattles is too busy filling his face with grain to notice. But if the capo catches him in the act, a very nasty fight will ensue. Like cockerels, pheasants have sharp spurs on their feet that can cause severe damage; it is at this point that the loser pheasant finds out that nature hasn't just endowed his rival with a superior pair of wattles, but also much bigger spurs.

The strange case of the homosexual necrophiliac duck

In 1995, Dutch researcher Kees Moeliker was sitting in his office in Rotterdam's Natural History Museum when a drake mallard crashed into the clear glass façade of the building and slumped to the ground dead. When Moeliker went outside a few minutes later to inspect the casualty, he was shocked to find another male mallard viciously pecking the back of its head. After a couple of minutes, this drake mounted the corpse and started to copulate furiously, pecking the dead duck's head as he did so. This continued for a full 75 minutes before Moeliker made his presence known, whereupon the necrophiliac drake ceased its morbid humping and waddled off to peck some grass. Moeliker was so astonished by what he had witnessed that he set out to investigate the science behind it, and earned himself the coveted Ig Nobel prize for improbable research in the biology category. Moeliker, now the museum's bird curator, believes the pair were engaged in a "rape flight attempt": a common phenomenon in the duck world where the male pursues another duck and forces it to mate. "Rape is a normal reproductive strategy in mallards," he was reported in the press as saying. "When one died the other one just went for it and didn't get any negative feedback – well, didn't get any feedback."

Can a bird be gay?

Homosexuality in animals is a controversial subject. Some people use the ambiguous evidence as proof that same-sex orientation is completely natural, others to show that it is completely not. You stride into the gay bird debate at your peril. To muddy the water still further, the really unhelpful answer to this question is: yes, no, maybe.

Homosexual behavior, but generally not sex, has been witnessed in a number of bird species. If a male does mount another male as if to copulate, it does so not to enjoy fulfilling sexual relations, as humans

IN THE GARDEN

Granny was wrong; bread is no good

For years people have been leaving out bread for their birds, but the current wisdom suggests we should think of alternatives. It's not that the bread is bad for birds, it just doesn't have much goodness. A bird that fills up on bread will be missing out on more nutritious foods.

might, but for one of a number of other reasons including mistaken identity ("Forgive me, I am SO sorry! From behind you're a dead ringer for my wife . . ."). Sometimes it will be an expression of sexual frustration when a male, after searching high and low, has been unable to find a mate. This is especially common among seabirds breeding in colonies in which there happen to be more males than females. There is, however, plenty of evidence of other homosexual behavior in birds, particularly among ducks, geese and swans. Roughly 25 percent of Australian black swan families are raised by

homosexual couples. One or both of two male black swans mate with a female then, once she's laid the eggs, chase her away, incubate the eggs themselves and bring up a family on their own. The good sense behind this evolutionary phenomenon is that two cobs, being a more powerful unit than a cob and a pen, can protect a larger territory and provide their brood with more to eat. Broods raised by a homosexual couple are more likely to survive than those raised by a heterosexual pair.

Roy and Silo, a pair of apparently gay chinstrap penguins in New York's Central Park Zoo, have found themselves at the heart of the animal homosexuality debate in recent years. In 1999, the two started "going out" and doing all the things that you'd expect a couple of gay penguins to do: vocalizing to one another, shunning female company and mounting each other. After they had unsuccessfully tried to incubate a rock, the chief zookeeper gave them a fertile egg to test their parenting skills. To the delight of many liberals, Roy and Silo successfully raised a female chick called Tango and, to their even greater delight, Tango came of age and promptly waddled off to pair up with another female called Tazuni. The less liberal members of the human community, keeping a watchful eye on developments at the zoo, grumbled that the homosexual bond only arose because the penguins were in captivity and not in their natural environment. They also pointed out that, in the wild, male chinstraps share the task of incubating the egg with the female, while in other penguin species the male does all the incubating. So, they concluded, there was no big deal about Roy and Silo sitting on a egg. But in 2005, the grumblers swapped popping their monocles for popping champagne corks when the shocking news leaked from the zoo that Silo had walked out on Roy for a hot Californian chick called Scrappy! The new couple made no attempt to hide their love for one another, hanging out by the pool, vocalizing and indulging in some heavy petting, while poor old Roy moped about looking miserable.

~~~~~~~~~

Use what talents you possess: the woods would be very silent if no birds sang there except those that sang best.

AUTHOR AND CLERGYMAN
HENRY VAN DYKE (1852–1933)

~~~~~~~~~

The wandering albatross, a model of fidelity

Most birds pair up with a mate for one breeding season and will grab a bit on the side when the other's not looking, but not so the wandering albatross, the most faithful of all birds, that will stay with its partner for the five or six decades of its life. These remarkable creatures, with the longest wingspan – 11 feet – of any bird, live on the wing for five to seven years after leaving the nest where they were born, on one of the sub-Antarctic islands. Not once do they touch the land as they circumnavigate the globe, skimming the frozen waters of the Southern Ocean from time to time to catch squid, octopus, cuttlefish and the offal thrown overboard by trawlermen. Held aloft by the powerful winds found in high southern latitudes, the wandering albatross can soar for hours without once having to go to the effort of flapping its wings. It will have circled the globe several dozen, even hundreds of times by the time it returns to land to find its life-long mate. For millions of years, the wandering albatross has been one of the few birds that dies of old age, but today it is far more likely to perish painfully on the baited hooks of an 80-mile-long line from a trawler emptying our oceans of tuna.

The intriguing sex life of the spotted sandpiper

The spotted sandpiper may be common and widespread across North America, but there is nothing conventional about the way it conducts its sexual affairs. Known by a variety of colloquial names, including teeter-peep, jerk bird and tip-tail, owing to the way it bobs and twitches, this little shorebird is one of just a handful of birds on the planet with reversed sex roles.

In complete contrast to the usual courtship arrangements in bird pairs, it is the female that is the more aggressive and active of the two while the male assumes the traditional parenting role of the female. Breaking with the usual pattern of avian breeding behavior, the female spotted sandpiper arrives before the male at the breeding grounds, stakes out its territory and sets about the exhausting daily business of showing off more impressively than her neighbors to attract a suitable partner – or rather, a series of partners. Her spirited courtship displays will sometimes lead to physical confrontations with rival females. (The larger female of the pair will defend her breeding patch every bit as vigorously as any male of other species.)

A shortage of available males is the reason why females become so aggressive. Early in the breeding season there are fewer males than females, but even when the males start to arrive in significant numbers, many disappear from circulation, leaving to incubate the clutches. In many breeding areas, at certain times of the season, there will be one male for every six females, and it's then that the feathers really start flying.

Compared to the female, the male spotted sandpiper has a higher level of pro-lactin, a pituitary hormone that encourages parental responsibility, so while he stays back at the nest to sit on the eggs or raise the young chicks, the female will be out playing the field with any half-fit male in the neighborhood. The female spotted sandpiper is known to mate with up to four other males in a breeding season, and, as she can

> Birds are born with a small bump, known as an egg tooth, on their bills to help them crack the eggshell when it's time to hatch. The tooth is shed soon afterward.

store sperm for up to four weeks, the eggs she lays for one male may well have been fertilized by a different male. From the Greek meaning "many husbands," or "men," this mating arrangement is known by scientists as *polyandry*. What makes spotted sandpipers especially intriguing to ornithologists is that in some breeding seasons, or in other areas, the pairs behave monogamously, and the females will help care for their young.

Wilson's phalarope, a small wader that breeds in the prairies, is the only other polyandrous bird in the United States.

A Cracking Start

RAISING THE FAMILY

Creating an egg is all in a day's work

The production of a bird egg is a remarkable and rapid business. The male's sperm fertilizes an ovum, or egg, which pushes through the ovary and sets off down the long tube of the oviduct developing, as it goes, the beginnings of the white (aka the albumen) and the yolk, which serves as the food source for the embryo – a source that in many cases is almost exhausted by the time the chick hatches. Three hours later, the egg moves into the uterus where a gland that secretes a lime compound (calcium carbonate mainly) will create the porous shell over the ensuing 20 hours. It is thought that the colors and markings of the eggshell are produced by bile pigments and the hemoglobin in blood. Thus it takes a mother bird just one day to

~~~~~~~~~

I'm youth, I'm joy, I'm a little bird that has broken out of the egg.

SCOTTISH NOVELIST SIR JAMES BARRIE (1860–1937)

~~~~~~~~~

create an ideal environment for her embryonic chick and a new life. Eggshells are porous and delicate so that the chicks can absorb oxygen through them and then peck their way out. White eggs are usually laid by birds safe from predators; the colored, speckled ones evolved as a camouflage for more vulnerable species. As a general rule, the more conspicuously colored the egg, the worse it tastes.

Unsuspecting foster parents

Coming from different families of birds and living on other sides of the planet, the cowbirds of the Americas and the cuckoos of Europe and Africa would appear to have little in common, but they share one very peculiar feature of behavior. They belong to a tiny group known as brood parasites, which lay their eggs in the nests of other species, abandoning their young to be brought up by unsuspecting "foster parents."

The brown-headed cowbird, a noisy character with a wide repertoire of songs and calls, used to be found only in the Great Plains where it followed bison herds, but, as forests have been cleared, it has spread in all directions and is now common across most of North America. This is partly due to the sheer number of eggs that the bird lays each year. Relieved of the tiresome chores of having to build a nest and feed her young, the female cowbird spends the warmer months courting males and dropping up to three dozen eggs a season into the nests of a staggering 220 species of birds. Some larger species of host birds destroy cowbird eggs or throw them out of the nest, but the majority don't notice the difference from their own.

Across the Atlantic, the cuckoo, an elusive dove-sized bird with the handsome looks of a bird of prey and a distinctive mellow song, performs similar raids on unsuspecting neighbors, usually dunnocks, meadow pipits, pied wagtails and reed warblers, whose eggs look very similar to her own so she can exploit their parental instincts to bring up her young. Like the cowbirds, cuckoo chicks always hatch first and then evict the eggs or young of the host bird, which will then feed the cuckoo chick as if it were her own – and all this while her own young lie splattered on the ground below. Both birds are only doing what all animals are programmed to do, namely whatever it takes to further the genetic line and produce as many young as they can. By laying their eggs in the nests of others, these remarkable birds are able to lay many more eggs than they would if they laid them in a nest of their own and had to go through the hassle of bringing the little critters up.

STATES/PROVINCES REPORTING THE MOST BIRD SPECIES

Rank	State/Province	Species
1	Texas	341
2	California	334
3	Florida	278
4	Arizona	254
5	Georgia	208
6	Washington	206
7	South Carolina	199
8	Oregon	197
9	British Columbia	193
9	North Carolina	193
9	New Mexico	193

Reported in the 2009 Great Backyard Bird Count, a joint project of the Cornell Lab of Ornithology and the National Audubon Society. During the annual four-day event, the continent's bird lovers count birds to create a real-time snapshot of bird concentrations.

Parents from hell

European coots make very strict parents. If one of the larger chicks becomes too demanding of food, or hostile toward its siblings, the parent will sometimes pick it up with its beak and give it a good shake, or even submerge it under water. Parental aggression is thought to reduce demands for feedings, giving the smaller chicks a fairer share. It also encourages independence. Occasionally, the admonished chick is so distraught by its rough treatment that it paddles away, never to return. Coots lay up to ten eggs, but only half the chicks – beautifully clothed in jet-black down with heads of bright orange, scarlet and purplish blue – will make it to adulthood.

I hope you love birds, too. It is economical. It saves going to Heaven.
EMILY DICKINSON (1830–86)

A very general opinion prevails that the brains and intestines of the Carolina Paroquet are a sure and fatal poison to cats. I had determined, when at Big Bone, to put this to the test of experiment; and for that purpose collected the brains and bowels of more than a dozen of them. But after close search, Mistress Puss was not to be found, being engaged, perhaps, on more agreeable business. I left the medicine with Mr. Colquhoun's agent to administer it at the first opportunity, and write me the result; but I have never yet heard from him. A respectable lady near the town of Natchez, and on whose word I can rely, assured me that she herself had made the experiment, and that, whatever might be the cause, the cat had actually died either on that or the succeeding day. A French planter near Bayou Fourche pretended to account to me for this effect by positively asserting that the seeds of the cockle burs, on which the Paroquets so eagerly feed, were deleterious to cats; and thus their death was produced by eating the intestines of the bird. These matters might easily have been ascertained on the spot, which, however, a combination of trifling circumstances prevented me from doing. I several times carried a dose of the first description in my pocket till it became insufferable, without meeting with a suitable patient on whom, like other professional gentlemen, I might conveniently make a fair experiment. . . .

❝ Since the foregoing was written, I have had an opportunity, by the death of a tame Carolina paroquet to ascertain the fact of the poisonous effects of their head and intestines on cats. Having shut up a cat and her two kittens (the latter only a few days old) in a room with the head, neck, and whole intestines, I found on the next morning, the whole eaten, except a small part of the bill. The cat exhibited no symptoms of sickness; and at this moment, three days after the experiment has been made, she and her kittens are in their usual health. Still, however, the effect might have been different, had the daily food of the birds been cockle burrs, instead of Indian corn. 🙶

**SCOTTISH ORNITHOLOGIST ANDREW WILSON,
AMERICAN ORNITHOLOGY, PUBLISHED 1808–14**

How to survive on a cold egg for four months

Emperor penguins breed during the coldest time of the year in the Antarctic when the wind-chill factor can send temperatures plunging to −76°F. Only a handful of animals on the planet are able to survive such conditions, let alone rear their young in them, but the penguins pull off this extraordinary feat using a host of tricks with which evolution has endowed them. After the entire colony has waddled up to 70 miles in from the edge of the ice pack, the female lays her egg and transfers it, often with great difficulty, onto the

~~~~~~~

Fall is my favorite season in Los Angeles, watching the birds change color and fall from the trees.

DAVID LETTERMAN (1947–)

~~~~~~~

feet of the male, desperately trying not to let it fall onto the ice where it would die in seconds. Handover complete, the female immediately disappears for up to two months in search of food that she will regurgitate for her newly hatched chick on her return. The male is left to incubate the egg, which he does by balancing it on his feet and covering it with a feathered "brood pouch." Emperor penguins are the sole species of bird where only the male incubates the egg:

IN THE GARDEN

Help birds to nest close to your home

Most birds start to build their nest in early spring in preparation for the breeding season.

Gather up some old **plant matter** from the garden, drying it out if necessary, and leave it in loose piles near hedges and under trees. Long grass, straw, hay, dead flower stems, twigs and small sticks will all be put to use.

Some birds, such as the house sparrow, will also use **fur, hair**, **wool** and other soft natural materials.

Don't throw away **fresh green leaves** pruned from shrubs in spring, or **moss** raked from your lawn, as starlings use these for their nests.

House martins, song thrushes and blackbirds need **mud** to construct their nests. The edge of a pond is ideal, but if the weather has been dry you can make your own wet, muddy patch by watering the odd corner of a flower bed.

for two months he just stands there getting battered and frozen by everything the Antarctic winter can throw at him. He is not alone by any means, but surrounded by thousands of other males, all huddling together to keep out the perishing wind. The huge commune slowly revolves and shuffles so that each gets a period in the warmth of the center. It takes up to three days for the chick to hatch. If it hatches before the mother has returned, the male feeds it a curd-like substance from a gland in his esophagus. When the females return (usually not later than two weeks after the chicks have hatched), each finds her partner without difficulty in the giant throng by recognizing his unique call. Then the starving males, who haven't eaten since the colony began their retreat to breed almost four months earlier, head off to the sea in search of a richly deserved meal of their own. Thereafter the parents take it in turns to forage and regurgitate food for the chick. When they are two and a half months old, the chicks congregate in a crèche, crowding together for warmth while their parents are hunting.

The Hen

Alas, my Child, where is the Pen
That can do Justice to the Hen?
Like Royalty, She goes her way,
Laying foundations every day,
Though not for Public Buildings, yet
For Custard, Cake and Omelette.
Or if too Old for such a use
They have their Fling at some Abuse,
As when to Censure Plays Unfit
Upon the Stage they make a Hit,
Or at elections Seal the Fate
Of an Obnoxious Candidate.
No wonder, Child, we prize the Hen,
Whose Egg is mightier than the Pen.

WRITER AND ARTIST OLIVER HERFORD (1863–1935)

Egg facts

- It would take 40 minutes to hard boil an ostrich egg.

- The extinct elephant bird of Madagascar laid the biggest eggs ever, weighing almost 28 pounds.

- The smallest egg of any living bird is that of the bee hummingbird, weighing half a gram – it would take 120 to match the weight of one standard hen's egg.

- The eggs of most garden birds are incubated for between 11 and 15 days.

Doing bird

The endangered great Indian hornbill, a strange-looking creature found in India and southeast Asia, grows up to four feet long and carries a highly distinctive and apparently useless "casque" of solid ivory on the upper part of its bill. Its breeding behavior is as odd as its appearance. When the female is ready to lay her eggs, she disappears into a hole in a tree that she seals up with a mixture of droppings, regurgitated food and earth brought by her partner, leaving a small slit through which he can continue to pass food and she can drop out her waste. Safe from predators, she stays in her birthing prison for three or four months until the chicks are well developed. In some species, the female breaks out of the structure earlier, and the chicks seal themselves in again, allowing both parents to forage and pass them food.

Puffin breeding facts

- They nest in burrows, some formerly occupied by rabbits, on clifftops.

- Parents take turns to incubate the one egg laid per season in 32-hour shifts.

- They feed the chick five or six times a day, flying up to 400 miles a day to find fish.

- They carry up to 20 small fish at a go in their colorful beaks when foraging for their chick.

- The parents are so tired (or should that be puffed?) from feeding the chick that they eventually give up, after about 40 days, and hunger forces the youngster to go and earn its own way in the world.

IN THE GARDEN

What to do if you find a baby bird

In late spring and early summer, when chicks are hatching and fledging, it is common to come across a baby bird on the ground. As the chicks grow, one may get accidentally nudged over the edge of the nest: if the one you find is covered in downy feathers, or is in a vulnerable position, such as the road or pavement, then it probably does need help and should be moved to the relative safety of nearby undergrowth. The advice is to put the bird as high up as possible out of the reach of predators, and as close to where you found it as possible so the parents can find and feed it. In the great majority of instances, however, the bird, no matter how terrified and vulnerable it looks, will be absolutely fine if it's left alone. More often than not, it is a fledgling about to take wing for the first time and the last thing it needs is a galumphing, well-meaning human clumsily trying to pick it up. The instinctive reaction of people who care about animals is to take some action, but often the wisest and kindest thing to do is to walk away. It's highly likely that the parents of the bird are very close by and probably even watching with mounting consternation as the caring human passerby tries to help out. If you're worried that the bird will be taken by a cat or other predator, the advice is to watch over it from a distance and shoo away the interloper.

The male bower-bird of Australia and New Guinea is one of the most fascinating creatures on the planet. The "bower" (nest) he builds to attract a female is a masterpiece of decoration, almost human in its artistry, detail and urgency to impress. After constructing a small hut out of twigs and branches, he sets about adorning the interior with colorful objects including flowers, feathers, fruit, shells, berries, stones, glass, plastic and paper. There are 18 species of bower-bird, and two of them, the satin and the regent, use leaves and twigs to paint the interior of the bowers with a dye made from chewed-up plants, charcoal and saliva. The building and decoration can take months and the bird will often move the objects around into different arrangements until he is perfectly happy. When the female tours the area to inspect the efforts of all the local suitors, the male performs a weird dance outside his bower, and in the case of some species will offer her one of his colorful objects as a love gift. Just as some of the dullest-looking birds are the best singers, it is the bower-bird species with the dreariest plumage that builds the most elaborate bowers. It's all about attracting a mate, whether you go in for singing beautifully, dressing up in sensational plumage, or showing off your interior design skills.

Cain and Abel

Most birds of prey lay two eggs, but can feed only one chick adequately; they will favor the first to hatch and effectively abandon the other. The elder sibling tends to bully the younger chick to death and then eat it – all with full parental approval – so that not a scrap of nutrition is wasted.

Coming of age is a leap in the dark

The cliff-dwelling guillemot lays one egg, shaped like a cone so that if it's nudged it's more likely to spin on the spot than roll off the edge. Unlike many birds, the guillemot can recognize its own egg and will return it to the nest if it has been moved. The chick hatches after four or five weeks and remains on the ledge of the cliff for about 16 days, waddling anxiously around and exercising its wings. Then one night the chick comes of age in dramatic fashion. Called by its parents from the water below, the chick leaps into darkness, hopefully tumbling harmlessly off the rocks and into the swelling sea. The parents then escort it further out to sea, feeding, teaching and caring for it, until it can fly and fish for itself. The chicks of the razorbill, the guillemot's cousin in the auk family, perform a similar rite of passage.

Sing a song of sixpence,
A pocket full of rye;
Four-and-twenty blackbirds
Baked in a pie!

When the pie was opened
The birds began to sing;
Was not that a dainty dish
To set before the king?

The king was in his counting-house,
Counting out his money;
The queen was in the parlour,
Eating bread and honey.

The maid was in the garden,
Hanging out the clothes;
When down came a blackbird
And snapped off her nose.

MEDIEVAL NURSERY RHYME

> **All songbirds emerge from the egg naked and blind. Some may say that that's just plain nidicolous.**

Can a swan really break our legs with its wings?

Swans can be very aggressive protecting their young and their territory, especially during the breeding season. Unlike most other animals, swans don't protect a square area but a linear one, a stretch of a lake or river, and woe betide anyone who glides into a cob's path when his cygnets are about. Rival cobs bear the brunt of their belligerence, but as any dog or canoeist will tell you, they're not the only ones at risk of a violent pecking. But the oft-repeated warning that a swan can break a human leg with a swipe of its wings is nonsense. Yes, it will hurt like hell and probably leave a bruise, but there is virtually no chance of it fracturing a healthy dense human bone, protected by flesh, muscle and clothing. The swan's own bones, though tough, are hollow and lightweight, like those of most birds, so that it can fly. A very elderly person with brittle bones, or a very small child, would feel a blow more keenly than others, but a fracture is still highly unlikely.

~~~~~~~~~~~~~~~~~~~~~~~~~~~~

The stately-sailing swan
Gives out his snowy plumage to the gale;
And, arching proud his neck, with oary feet
Bears forward fierce, and guards his osier isle,
Protective of his young.

SCOTTISH POET JAMES THOMSON (1700–48)

~~~~~~~~~~~~~~~~~~~~~~~~~~~~

How long can a bird expect to live?

It varies greatly between the species but most birds we see in our gardens will do well to reach their first birthday, the majority falling victim to predators or starvation. Broadly speaking, the larger the bird, the longer the life. Birds of prey, who are rarely preyed upon themselves except by humans, can live for 20 or 30 years; and many seabirds, which have a very low annual death rate of under 10 percent, will also make it into their twenties. Parrots and albatrosses are the longest-living, often reaching a fifth, sixth or even seventh decade. Waders live between five and 10 years. Garden birds such as robins, sparrows, tits and finches generally have a life span of one or two, though in rare cases that can stretch to eight. Roughly 75 percent of the population of small garden birds dies in the course of every year.

Is there a pecking order in bird communities?

Among birds that feed in groups or flocks there is a ranking system that is represented in the bird's markings. The older, stronger, more dominant bird gets the best seat at the bird table, while the younger, weaker ones have to scrap for the leftovers. Once the dominant bird has eaten its fill and moves off to preen itself, copulate or just sit back and enjoy the view from a nearby branch, those that remain at the feeding site are more vulnerable to predators as there are fewer eyes on the lookout. The young and the frail are therefore at greater risk; it is a case of the survival of the strongest. Birds may look cute, but there's not a charitable or altruistic feather on their bodies. Several sparrow species, yellow warbler and the great tit – the European cousin of the chickadee and the titmouse – have come to establish their position in the pecking order by displaying their rank, just like soldiers, with stripes of darker feathers: the widest denoting the most senior. What no bird can afford to do if it can help it is waste time fighting over feed, which both burns up valuable energy and distracts the attention from outside dangers. Nature has worked out that there's no point in throwing haymakers in the shrubbery over a couple of grass seeds when Tiddles the cat is on the prowl.

The Thrush's Nest

Within a thick and spreading hawthorn bush
   That overhung a molehill large and round,
I heard from morn to morn a merry thrush
   Sing hymns to sunrise, and I drank the sound
With joy; and, often, an intruding guest,
   I watched her secret toil from day to day –
How true she warped the moss to form a nest,
   And modelled it within with wood and clay;
And by and by, like heath-bells gilt with dew,
   There lay her shining eggs, as bright as flowers,
Ink-spotted over shells of greeny blue;
   And there I witnessed, in the sunny hours,
A brood of nature's minstrels chirp and fly,
   Glad as that sunshine and the laughing sky.

ENGLISH POET JOHN CLARE (1793–1864)

Superlative birds

Smallest: bee hummingbird: 2 inches long and weighing about 1/10 ounce

Heaviest flying bird: kori bustard and great bustard: can weigh upward of 40 pounds

Heaviest: ostrich: average weight 198–287 pounds, maximum 344 pounds

Tallest: ostrich: 5.9–8.9 feet

Longest wingspan: wandering albatross: 11.2 feet or more

Longest bill: Australian pelican: 19 inches

Fastest flying: peregrine falcon: 112 mph (when diving)

Slowest: American woodcock: 5 mph

Fastest wingbeat: hummingbird

Longest soaring: albatross and condor

Longest airborne seabird: sooty tern: 3 to 10 years without landing

Longest airborne land bird: swift: three years without landing

Longest two-way migration: Arctic tern: 24,980 miles

Strongest sense of smell: kiwi

Keenest sense of hearing: barn owl

Best eyesight: owls and other birds of prey

Most intelligent: African gray parrot and crow

Most talkative: African gray parrot

Fastest running: ostrich: 43 mph

Fastest underwater swimmer: gentoo penguin: 40 mph

Deepest diver: emperor penguin: 1,800 feet

Longest underwater: emperor penguin: 18 minutes

Coldest temperature endured: snowy owl: −80.5°F

Greatest weight-carrying capacity: bald eagle or pallas fish eagle: can lift 14 pounds

Longest without eating: male emperor penguin: 3–4 months when incubating

Most northerly nesting: ivory gull: at edge of Arctic Circle ice sheet

Largest nest: social weavers: 300-chamber "apartment" nests 26 feet long and 7 feet high

Worst-smelling nest: Eurasian hoopoe

Largest egg: ostrich: 7 inches by 5.5 inches

Largest clutch by a nidicolous (born naked and blind) species: blue tit: 19 eggs

Largest clutch by a nidifugous (born downy and active) species: bobwhite quail: 28 eggs

Largest average clutch size: gray partridge: 15–19

Smallest clutch: albatross: one egg every two years

Longest uninterrupted incubation period: emperor penguin: 65 days

Shortest incubation period: small songbirds: 11 days

Longest fledging period of flying birds: wandering albatross: 270 days

Fastest to breeding maturity: common quail: five weeks

Slowest to breeding maturity: royal albatross and wandering albatross: 6–10 years

Longest-lived wild bird: albatross: upwards of 60 years

Country with most endangered species: Indonesia: 130

Country with the highest percentage of its species endangered: New Zealand: 30 percent

ADVICE ON WHAT FOOD
TO OFFER YOUR BIRDS

Sunflower. Black sunflower seeds are an excellent all-year food. The oil content is higher in black than in striped ones, which makes them more nutritious. Shelled sunflower hearts are better still because they are easier to eat, leave no mess and are more hygienic. The birds don't have to break open the casings, which can become an avian health hazard lying below a feeder covered in disease-riddled waste.

Safflower. This white seed, high in protein and fat, will attract plenty of backyard favorites, while deterring unwanted guests such as starlings, grackles and squirrels. Cardinals, chickadees, nuthatches, titmice, finches and grosbeaks love safflower seeds.

Suet. Woodpeckers, nuthatches, bluebirds, chickadees and many other species love suet especially in the winter when its high fat content helps boost flagging energy levels. You can buy commercial suet cakes or make your own (see page 122).

Nuts. Raw nuts are a great winter food because they are rich in calories and fat. Salted or dry-roasted peanuts should not be used.

Niger seed. This tiny black seed, which needs a special feeder with small feeding holes, is great for attracting goldfinches and pine siskin.

Sugar water. Hummingbirds, robins, grosbeaks, blue jays, cardinals, finches, woodpeckers and chickadees are just a few of many birds that flock to sugar water feeders.

Mealworms. Orioles, bluebirds, warblers, purple martins, thrushes and many other birds love fresh mealworms, which can be bought at fish bait shops as well as pet stores. Mealworms can be expensive to buy and many people now grow their own. It is very important to make sure the mealworms are fresh because dead or rancid ones can cause salmonella poisoning and other illnesses.

Fresh coconut in the shell. Rinse out any residues of the sweet coconut water from the middle of the coconut before hanging it out to prevent the buildup of black mildew.

Cooked rice, brown or white (without added salt) is beneficial and readily accepted by all species during severe winter weather. Uncooked rice may be eaten by birds such as pigeons, doves and pheasants but is less likely to attract other species.

ADVICE ON WHAT FOOD
NOT TO OFFER YOUR BIRDS

Salted foods that birds can't digest and that damage the nervous system.

Some peanuts can be high in a natural poison that can kill birds, so buy from a reputable dealer who will guarantee their nuts don't contain aflatoxin.

Wheat and barley grains are often included in commercial seed mixtures, but they are really only suitable for pigeons, doves and pheasants, which feed on the ground and rapidly increase in numbers, deterring the smaller species.

Avoid seed mixtures that have **split peas, beans, dried rice** or **lentils** as only the larger species can eat them dry. These are added to some cheaper seed mixes to bulk them up.

Polyunsaturated margarines or vegetable oils. These are unsuitable for birds. Unlike humans, birds need high levels of saturated fat, such as found in raw suet and lard. Moreover the soft fats can easily get smeared onto the feathers, destroying their waterproofing and insulating qualities.

Dry biscuit is not recommended as birds may choke on the hard lumps. It is sometimes added to cheaper seed mixtures for bulk – look out for green or pink lumps, and avoid any mixture containing them. Soaked dog biscuit is excellent, except in hot weather as it quickly dries out. Petfood may attract larger birds such as magpies and gulls, and also neighborhood cats, so don't use it if that happens.

Never give **milk** to any bird. They're not designed to digest milk, which will cause serious illness and even death.

Desiccated coconut should never be used as it may swell once inside a bird and kill it.

Porridge oats must never be cooked as this makes them glutinous and they may harden around a bird's beak.

Moldy and stale food. While many molds are harmless, there are some that can cause respiratory infections in birds, so it is best to be cautious and avoid moldy food entirely. If food turns moldy or stale on your bird table, you are probably putting out too large a quantity for the birds to eat in one day. Always remove any decaying food as it provides a breeding ground for salmonella food-poisoning bacteria.

Love and War

WHY BIRDS SING AND CALL

Why do birds sing?
And why is it only the males?

When we lie in bed in the morning as the watery late winter sun seeps through our curtains, the mad chattering of the birds outside tells us that the avian world is alive once again with the frenetic business of breeding. It's the males making all the noise, prompted by the rising level of testosterone in their bodies, and they have only two things on their mind as they squawk and tweet and chirrup: love and war. The signature song of a male songbird has a twin purpose: to attract a female and to deter a male rival from entering his territory and trying to pull his bird. Females don't need to sing because they're the ones that do the choosing. (Female European robins are an exception to this rule, noisily defending their own territory outside of the breeding season.) Females judge the complexity and quality of his song to weigh up a male's potential fitness as a partner.

You may have noticed that for the second half of the year your garden is a fairly quiet place, compared with the musical maelstrom filling the air for the first six months. That's because our birds don't breed in the autumn and winter, and so there's little reason to sing. Most of the noises birds make at this time are calls, not songs. The breeding season begins in late winter, reaches a noisy climax in May, and peters out in June and July after the chicks have fledged and the exhausted parents can finally ease up a little.

Often each male has characteristic features to his songs so that every individual sounds fractionally different. Each can therefore recognize the songs of his neighbors, who have also settled down with a mate and thus pose no threat. This means he doesn't have to waste valuable energy, at an especially energy-sapping period of the year, erupting into his "Oi-you!-get-out-of-my-bush-leave-my bird-alone!" routine every time his neighbor has a quick chirrup. It is only when a stranger, an unattached male from another area, turns up that he has to go to the lung-busting effort of warning him off.

The principle holds true for the most part that the plainer the bird, the better it sings. And vice versa, the more colorful the bird, the worse it sings (witness the peacock).

A Bird's Anger

A summer's morning that has but one voice;
Five hundred stooks, like golden lovers, lean
Their heads together, in their quiet way,
And but one bird sings, of a number seen.

It is the lark, that louder, louder sings,
As though but this one thought possessed his mind:
"You silent robin, blackbird, thrush, and finch,
I'll sing enough for all you lazy kind!"

And when I hear him at this daring task,
"Peace, little bird," I say, "and take some rest;
Stop that wild, screaming fire of angry song,
Before it makes a coffin of your nest."

WELSH POET W. H. DAVIES (1871–1940)

What's the difference between a call and a song?

A call is uttered by females as well as males. The ability to call is genetically inherited, not learned. A call is short and to the point, e.g., "Get the hell out of that bird bath, Socks the cat is about." A song is more complex, longer and sung only by the males to attract a female mate or warn off rival males from their territory. Many birds that don't sing, such as gulls and parrots, have complex repertoires of calls. All birds can call or make a noise, but it's only the passerines, or songbirds, that sing.

It's *passerine* to you, pal

"Passerine" refers to birds with three toes pointing forward and one pointing backward, but to you and me it is just a fancy word for "songbird." If you want to impress someone with your intelligence, say to them, by way of a conversation starter: "I can't tell you how beautifully the passerines in my garden were vocalizing this morning." There are over 4,000 passerines, almost half the bird species in the world. All common garden birds are passerines, except for the wood pigeon and collared dove.

World in harmony

Insomniacs may beg to differ, but the dawn chorus is one of the great wonders of nature. It is a sound that has been heard around the world from, well, the dawn of time, and in all environments: European and North American woods, tropical rain forest, African savannahs . . . But quite why songbirds put on such a magnificent choral performance each spring morning before the sun rises is still something of a mystery. For a start, it should be noted that there's little else to do at that time of the day if you're a bird. Foraging for food is not an option as seeds and insects are more difficult to find in the gloom and there is a greater risk of being taken by a predator. (Cats do most of their hunting at dawn and dusk when the light is poor.) As so often with birds, there seems to be more than one explanation. One is that sound travels as much as 20 times more effectively at daybreak since there is little other noise and generally little wind, but the main reason seems to be that the males (who do all the singing) see dawn as a perfect opportunity, in what will soon become a busy day of feeding, preening and cat-dodging, to attract a female. A cold night of sitting in a bush with no food since the evening before greatly depletes a bird's energy reserves. The hearty early morning choristers, all desperately trying to out-sing their love rivals, are thus sending out a statement of their machismo and their fitness as a partner: "Hey, darling, check *me* out. I may be exhausted and freezing but I can still bust a big tune for you."

Some birds, though, notably the nightingale, have become fed up with all the early morning competition for the airwaves and have evolved the cunning trick of doing most of their singing by night.

Then from the neighboring thicket the mockingbird,
    wildest of singers,
Swinging aloft on a willow spray that hung o'er the water,
Shook from his little throat such floods of delirious music,
That the whole air and the woods and the waves seemed
    silent to listen.

POET HENRY WADSWORTH LONGFELLOW (1807–82)

Bird song varies enormously, according to habitat. Thrushes, blackbirds, nightingales and other woodland species have rich, loud, complex songs so they can be heard through dense foliage. Birds living in flat marshland, by contrast, have simple, repetitive songs suited to the open, uncluttered surroundings.

Let me be to Thee as the circling bird,
Or bat with tender and air-crisping wings
That shapes in half-light his departing rings,
From both of whom a changeless note is heard.
I have found my music in a common word,
Trying each pleasurable throat that sings
And every praisèd sequence of sweet strings,
And know infallibly which I preferred.

The authentic cadence was discovered late
Which ends those only strains that I approve,
And other science all gone out of date
And minor sweetness scarce made mention of:
I have found the dominant of my range and state –
Love, O my God, to call Thee Love and Love.

ENGLISH POET GERARD MANLEY HOPKINS (1844–89)

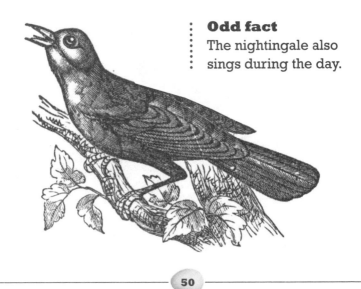

Odd fact
The nightingale also
sings during the day.

Birds named after the sound they make

Cuckoo
Chiffchaff
Whipoorwill
Macaw
Hoopoe
Chough
Crake
Kittiwake
Pipit
Shrike
Twite
Whimbrel
Whooper swan

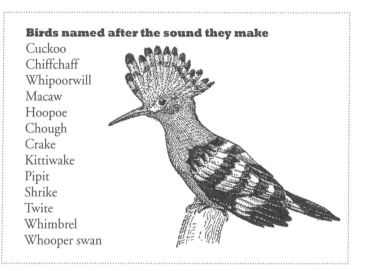

Alwite, me old cock sparrer?

Many species of birds communicate in dialects peculiar to their area. Males do this because a female is more likely to be attracted to a bird familiar with local conditions than any old johnny-fly-by-night passing through. As with human communities, some local dialects are much stronger than others, making them almost unrecognizable to other members of the species from other areas.

❝ 'An abode without birds is like meat without seasoning.' Such was not my abode for I found myself suddenly neighbor to the birds; not by having imprisoned one, but having caged myself near them. I was not only nearer to some of those which commonly frequent the garden and the orchard, but to those wilder and more thrilling songsters of the forest which, rarely, or never serenade a villager. ❞

HENRY DAVID THOREAU, *WALDEN, OR LIFE IN THE WOODS*

Breaking news . . .

There is truth in the saying that the early bird catches the worm because thrushes, robins, bluebirds and skylarks, all of whom enjoy a worm for breakfast, are among the earliest risers.

Front row seat

If you want to go outdoors to listen to a dawn chorus in all its glory, rather than one muffled by curtains, walls and earplugs, then check the weather forecast, wait for a fine, clear morning with next to no wind and head into a secluded spot in your garden or beyond to an area with an even larger concentration of songbirds. Late April to early June is the best period, when summer visitors have added their voices to those of the permanent residents. Dawn chorus begins an hour before sunrise, peaks 30 minutes later and ends half an hour after sun-up.

> **Best singers**
> Warblers
> Thrushes
> Nightingales
> Winter wren
> Skylarks
> Mockingbirds

" Though I know something about British birds I should have been lost and confused among American birds, of which unhappily I know little or nothing. Colonel Roosevelt not only knew more about American birds than I did about British birds, but he knew about British birds also. What he had lacked was an opportunity of hearing their songs, and you cannot get a knowledge of the songs of birds in any other way than by listening to them.

. . . We began our walk, and when a song was heard I told him the name of the bird. I noticed that as soon as I mentioned the name it was unnecessary to tell him more. He knew what the bird was like. It was not necessary for him to see it. He knew the kind of bird it was, its habits and appearance. He just wanted to complete his knowledge by hearing the song. He had, too, a very trained ear for bird songs, which cannot be acquired without having spent much time in listening to them. How he had found time in that busy life to acquire this knowledge so thoroughly it is almost impossible to imagine, but there the knowledge and training undoubtedly were. He had one of the most perfectly trained ears for bird songs that I have ever known, so that if three or four birds were singing together he would pick out their songs, distinguish each, and ask to be told each separate name; and when farther on we heard any bird for a second time, he would remember the song from the first telling and be able to name the bird himself. "

SIR EDWARD GREY, BRITISH FOREIGN SECRETARY 1905–16, OF HIS CLOSE FRIEND AND FELLOW BIRD ENTHUSIAST PRESIDENT TEDDY ROOSEVELT

Why does the garden go so quiet at the end of the summer?

At the end of the breeding season, birds are exhausted, disheveled and in need of a change of scenery. Many birds have made tens, even hundreds of thousands of trips in and out of bushes and hedges to feed their chicks, leaving their feathers in need of renewal. When they lose their feathers, they are more vulnerable to predators because they cannot fly so well. While their plumage regenerates, they keep their heads down. Another reason behind their silence is that once the breeding season is over, males no longer need to sing to attract a mate or defend a territory, and the family no longer needs its nest once the chicks have fledged and set out on their own.

Late summer and early autumn is also harvest time when food is in abundant supply for birds as well as people, so many birds leave their breeding grounds to enjoy the berries and seeds on offer in farmland, orchards and woods.

~~~~~~~~~

The language of birds is very ancient, and, like other ancient modes of speech, very elliptical: little is said, but much is meant.

GILBERT WHITE

~~~~~~~~~

I take my joy in the cry of the gannet
And the sound of the curlew
Instead of the laughter of men;
The singing of the gull
Instead of the drinking of mead.

FROM *THE SEAFARER*, OLD ENGLISH POEM, AUTHOR AND DATE UNKNOWN

❝ The skylark is so universally diffused in these islands, and so abundant, well known and favourite a species, that anything beyond a brief and prosaic account of its habits would appear superfluous. His image, better than any portray it, already exists in every mind. A distinguished ornithologist, writing of the sparrow, declines to describe its language, and asks his reader to open his window and hear it for himself. In like manner, I may ask the reader to listen to the lark's song, which exists registered in his own brain. For he must have heard it times without number, this being a music which, like the rain and sunshine, falls on all of us. If someone, too curious, should desire me not to concern myself with the images and registered sensations of others' brains, but to record here my own impressions and feelings, I could but refer him to Shelley's 'Ode to a Skylark,' which describes the bird at its best – the bird, and the feeling produced on the listener. Some ornithologist (I blush to say it) has pointed out that the poet's description is unscientific and of no value; nevertheless, it embodies what we all feel at times, although we may be without inspiration, and have only dull prose for expression. It is true that there are those who are not moved by nature's sights and sounds, even in her special moments, who regard a skylark merely as something to eat with a delicate flavour. It is well, if we desire to think the best we can of our fellows, to look on such persons as exceptions, like those, perhaps fabled, monsters of antiquity who feasted on nightingales' tongues and other strange meats. ❞

BRITISH NATURALIST AND ORNITHOLOGIST W. H. HUDSON (1841–1922)

To a Skylark

Hail to thee, blithe Spirit!
Bird thou never wert –
That from Heaven or near it
Pourest thy full heart
In profuse strains of unpremeditated art.

Higher still and higher
From the earth thou springest,
Like a cloud of fire;
The blue deep thou wingest,
And singing still dost soar, and soaring ever singest.

In the golden lightning
Of the sunken sun,
O'er which clouds are bright'ning,
Thou dost float and run,
Like an unbodied joy whose race is just begun.

The pale purple even
Melts around thy flight;
Like a star of heaven,
In the broad daylight
Thou art unseen, but yet I hear thy shrill delight –

Keen as are the arrows
Of that silver sphere
Whose intense lamp narrows
In the white dawn clear,
Until we hardly see, we feel that it is there.

All the earth and air
With thy voice is loud,
As, when night is bare,
From one lonely cloud
The moon rains out her beams, and Heaven is overflow'ed.

What thou art we know not;
What is most like thee?
From rainbow clouds there flow not
Drops so bright to see,
As from thy presence showers a rain of melody: –

Like a poet hidden
In the light of thought,
Singing hymns unbidden,
Till the world is wrought
To sympathy with hopes and fears it heeded not:

Like a high-born maiden
In a palace tower,
Soothing her love-laden
Soul in secret hour
With music sweet as love, which overflows her bower:

Like a glow-worm golden
In a dell of dew,
Scattering unbeholden
Its aërial hue
Among the flowers and grass which screen it from the view:

Like a rose embower'd
In its own green leaves,
By warm winds deflower'd,
Till the scent it gives
Makes faint with too much sweet these heavy-wingèd thieves:

Sound of vernal showers
On the twinkling grass,
Rain-awaken'd flowers –
All that ever was
Joyous and clear and fresh – thy music doth surpass.

Teach us, sprite or bird,
What sweet thoughts are thine:
I have never heard
Praise of love or wine
That panted forth a flood of rapture so divine.

Chorus hymeneal,
Or triumphal chant,
Match'd with thine would be all
But an empty vaunt –
A thing wherein we feel there is some hidden want.

What objects are the fountains
Of thy happy strain?
What fields, or waves, or mountains?
What shapes of sky or plain?
What love of thine own kind? what ignorance of pain?

With thy clear keen joyance
Languor cannot be:
Shadow of annoyance
Never came near thee:
Thou lovest, but ne'er knew love's sad
    satiety.

Waking or asleep,
Thou of death must deem
Things more true and deep
Than we mortals dream,
Or how could thy notes flow in such a crystal stream?

We look before and after,
And pine for what is not:
Our sincerest laughter
With some pain is fraught;
Our sweetest songs are those that tell of saddest thought.

Yet, if we could scorn
Hate and pride and fear,
If we were things born
Not to shed a tear,
I know not how thy joy we ever should come near.

Better than all measures
Of delightful sound,
Better than all treasures
That in books are found,
Thy skill to poet were, thou scorner of the ground!

Teach me half the gladness
That thy brain must know;
Such harmonious madness
From my lips would flow,
The world should listen then, as I am listening now.

ENGLISH POET PERCY BYSSHE SHELLEY (1792–1822)

Making an internal call

The chicks of European quail, American white pelican, guillemot, stone curlew and several species of duck and goose can call out before they have hatched. The quails call to each other to arrange a simultaneous hatching. As the eight eggs in the nest are incubated at the same time, there is a danger that the first of these precocial birds to hatch would stray off before the others had appeared, making them vulnerable to predators. To avoid this, evolution has granted them the ability to communicate and hatch within no more than six hours of one another. It may also be that the family members get to learn each other's voices from the outset in order to find each other more easily in the thick ground vegetation where they roam. The American white pelican chick calls from inside the shell to tell its parent that it is either too hot or too cold. A number of female ducks also exchange calls with their unhatched ducklings in order to teach them homing and distress calls vital for their survival.

~~~~~~~~~~~~~~~~~~~~~~~~~

Be grateful for luck. Pay the thunder no mind –
listen to the birds. And don't hate nobody.

JAZZ COMPOSER EUBIE BLAKE (1887–1973)

~~~~~~~~~~~~~~~~~~~~~~~~~

IN THE GARDEN

Clean bird feeders in late summer

Many birds disappear from our gardens in the second half of the summer, at the end of the breeding season, to take advantage of all the seeds, berries, grains and fruits available around harvest time not just on farmland but also on scrubland and roadside verges. This "vacation" provides a perfect opportunity to give an extra-thorough scrub-down to feeders and bird tables before the birds start to return in great numbers around the time of the first frosts. This cleansing is vital to help reduce the spread of disease among birds.

Let the feeders soak for a few minutes in a solution of nine parts water to one part of a disinfectant, such as bleach (or you can buy special bird-feeder solution) and then scrub them with a brush before rinsing them thoroughly and leaving them to dry (a wire-stemmed brush is ideal for tube feeders). It's a good idea to clean feeders as often as possible throughout the year, perhaps rotating them with others, so that there is a constant supply of food. Bird tables and baths should be cleared of debris every day and scrubbed once a week as they are likely to contain droppings, which pass on many common avian diseases. You should always wear gloves when washing feeders, tables or water containers. It's also important to move feeders and tables to different positions in the garden, perhaps every two weeks, to prevent the build-up of disease-carrying material on the ground below.

Why Don't Birds Wee?

BIRDS AND THEIR BODIES

Why do birds molt?

Without a full set of good quality feathers a bird will soon die. Birds suffer a lot of wear and tear in their everyday lives and that eventually takes its toll on their plumage. They fly in and out of bushes or reeds, getting snagged by branches, twigs and thorns, they are constantly exposed to the elements and they are riddled with parasites, which they often try to pick or rub off. A bird's plumage has to be in good condition in order for it to be able to fly efficiently, which it needs to do to gather its daily quota of food and to avoid being caught by a predator. Furthermore, birds must maintain a very high body temperature and they can't have shabby feathers undermining their insulation. Many male birds also attract a mate by having the best plumage in town, transforming themselves into colorful, immaculately presented creatures at the start of the breeding season. As any peacock will tell you, scruffy birds don't cut it. Males aren't going to throw away millions of years of hard evolutionary work with some slack grooming.

The depths to which emperors will sink

It is easy to forget that penguins are birds, since they can't fly and they spend more time in the water than they do on the land. Emperor penguins, in particular, seem to have more in common with the fish they eat than with their feathered cousins. Holding their breath for up to 20 minutes, emperors can dive up to 1,800 feet deeper than any other bird, and deeper than the height of the Empire State Building. Mostly they stay within 650 feet of the surface to find fish, squid and krill to eat, but if need be, their extraordinary physiology allows them to plunge to far greater depths in the freezing waters of the Southern Ocean around Antarctica. Emperors, the largest of the penguins with an average height of 3 feet 9 inches and weight of 70 pounds, have a highly efficient form of hemoglobin that makes use of every last iota of available oxygen. After a particularly deep dive, they have virtually no oxygen left in their respiratory system or blood but the vital organs still operate long after they would have packed up in any other animal. To help preserve oxygen, the emperors' heart rate can drop to just five or six beats per minute.

Why do the birds we eat have white and dark meat?

The most active muscles of edible birds are full of blood vessels so that they receive a lot of oxygen. These become dark, while the less active, better rested muscles remain white. Turkeys, chickens, quail, pheasants and other gallinaceous birds spend most of their time running on the ground, so their legs and thighs produce the darkest meat. The breast muscles of these birds, which are used for flying, are exercised very rarely, so the meat is white.

Some of my best friends are vultures

The vulture is an ugly bird with terrible table manners that wees on itself and eats dead bodies. It also has a charmless habit of vomiting a foul-smelling gunk over any other animal stupid enough to prey upon it. It is not difficult to see how it has never won a place in our hearts: "Vulture, Queen of Birds" will never sound right. The vulture is a fascinating creature, however, and it has more human friends than you might have thought, given its etiquette issues. It operates in extreme temperatures. High up in the sky, where the vultures soar and scan the horizon for prey, it is bitterly cold and they have thick plumage to keep themselves warm, but down on the ground, especially in Africa and Asia, the temperature can be overwhelmingly hot. To help them cool down, they have developed a technique, known as urohydrosis, of spraying urine on themselves, which then evaporates. (Storks also do this.) The urine also has a sterilizing effect, killing off any germs they may have picked up from the rotten carcasses on which they have fed. In recent years, this unloved bird has attracted a growing band of admirers and supporters in the United States, where the populations of the two species found there, the turkey vulture and the black vulture, have been growing sharply. More cars means more roadkill means more vultures, but more roadkill also means more germs and diseases. The vultures have earned the nickname "Nature's garbage disposal system" as a tribute to the way they clear up all the carcasses on the nation's roads.

Why do birds lay eggs and not give birth like the rest of us warm-blooded vertebrates?

A bird needs to fly to survive and to fly it needs to be as light as possible for as long as possible. Incredibly, it takes a bird just 24 hours to produce and lay an egg, but this speed is very sensible because it means that the bird is never grounded and can continue to search for food and flee from predators. A bird would barely get airborne if it had evolved to carry its young around inside it. Imagine a heavily pregnant female human trying to sprint 100 yards and then do the high jump. You get the picture. The avian system of laying and then incubating an egg also means that the female can rope the male into a much greater share of the work involved in reproduction: helping with duties around the nest, including taking his turn to sit on the eggs and later tend to the hatchlings.

Why don't vultures have feathers on their head and neck?

Vultures feed by sticking their heads into carcasses, covering head and neck in blood, fat and entrails. So evolution has removed the boring job of cleaning them by getting rid of the feathers altogether.

Grit to the mill

It's easy to see why so many birds are happy to eat seeds and nothing but seeds. Seeds are nature's power food, crammed with goodness and energy to help them transform into young plants with the potential to grow dozens of feet into the air and/or bear pounds and pounds of fruit. But plants guard their offspring every bit as zealously as animals, encasing their seeds in tough outer shells to give them a chance of surviving. In response, birds have acquired powerful beaks and remarkable digestive systems, as well as the skills to pry out the goodness from the seeds and nuts. In the absence of teeth to do the grinding, the stomachs of seed-eating birds such as sparrows and pigeons have evolved into highly effective milling machines, which pro-

duce digestive juices in a first chamber, then churn the seeds with the powerful muscles of the second chamber, in the gizzard. To help the milling process, the birds also eat dozens, even hundreds, of small bits of grit. In larger seed-eaters like chickens, turkeys and, at the extreme end of the scale, the flightless ostrich, the gizzard is bigger and holds more grit because such birds don't have to worry about being too heavy to get airborne.

An ostrich at the London Zoo was once found to have swallowed an alarm clock, a roll of film, a handkerchief, a piece of rope, a cycle valve, a pencil, three gloves, a collar stud, a Belgian franc, and a bunch of coins. Most ostriches in the wild settle for small stones to help them digest not only seeds but also crunchy insects and tougher vegetable matter such as the pods of the acacia tree and aloe plants.

Feathers are what make birds unique

No other creature has them. Others can fly (insects, bats, some squirrels, some lizards), others lay eggs (reptiles, fishing insects and two weird mammals), and plenty of other creatures are warm-blooded vertebrates. Feathers are the one feature that makes a bird unlike any other living thing.

Do birds get fat?

Fat birds don't make great fliers so most are programmed to stay trim in order to maintain their aviation efficiency. Birds also burn up calories at an incredibly fast rate in their manic, energy-sapping lifestyle. Flying, in particular, is an exhausting business and as birds spend much of their day in the air looking for food they are burning off energy almost as quickly as they're consuming it. The sedentary life is not an option for birds. Whereas many mammals can go weeks without food, most birds will die within a few days. Starvation is the biggest cause of death among birds, even in countries like Britain that are comparatively rich in plants and insects, and in rodents for the birds of prey. There simply isn't enough food to go round. In most bird species, those who live in an area rich in food sources are the lucky minority.

Migratory birds, however, are the exceptions to the rule that birds don't get fat. Swallows, swifts and martins eat insects on the wing as they travel back and forth between southern Africa and Europe, so their weight never changes significantly, but other migratory birds, especially waders, put on huge amounts of fat to sustain them on their long journeys. Fat makes an excellent fuel because it is lighter than carbohydrate and protein and, pound for pound, the bird gets twice as much energy from it. As the time to migrate approaches, birds go into an eating frenzy triggered by an automatic increase in appetite. This gorging process, known as hyperphagia, begins about two to three weeks before the birds take wing for foreign climes, increasing their weight by about 2 percent per day – though some birds can pile on as much as 10 percent by the time the sun sets. At the same time, changes in the bird's physiology improve the way they produce and store fat.

Birds that don't migrate usually carry about 3 to 5 percent fat; birds flying shorter distances need a "fat load" of between 10 and 25 percent; while the longer-distance migrants need anywhere between 40 percent and, in the case of some warblers, a scales-busting 100 percent, to give them the energy they need for their epic transcontinental flights. These birds hit their weight limits shortly before setting out over the most challenging geographical features of their journey, such as deserts, mountain ranges, oceans and seas.

Penguins are probably the birds with the most consistently high fat level because, having evolved into aquatic creatures no longer needing to fly, there's no reason for them to be light. On the contrary, given the temperatures they have to withstand, the more fat the better to insulate them and to enable them to survive sometimes prolonged periods without food.

Why don't woodpeckers get headaches or knock themselves out?

When a woodpecker hammers away at a tree trunk to search for insects or to mark out its territory – hundreds of times per minute in some species – the blows from its chisel-like beak crack into the wood at roughly 20 mph. In other birds, just one blow of such force would be enough to render them unconscious, but the woodpecker has evolved a highly efficient system for stopping the shock passing straight to its brain. The skull is much thicker than in other birds and its small brain is positioned better to withstand the repeated shocks. The bones connecting the beak to the skull are not as solid and inflexible, and the joints are connected with elastic, highly malleable tissues. Strong neck muscles provide the force for drilling while also absorbing some of the shock. In a neat finish to its physiological design, evolution has endowed the woodpecker with stiff little feathers to shield its nostrils from the flying debris, while its eyes produce a coating of thick membrane that acts like a pair of workman's goggles.

> A bird came down the walk
> He did not know I saw
> He bit an angleworm in halves
> And ate the fellow raw.
>
> **EMILY DICKINSON**

Why do beaks come in so many different shapes and sizes?

All beaks have evolved to help birds catch their food in the most suitable way possible. Birds of prey have short, sharp, hooked beaks ideal for ripping flesh; finches and sparrows have short, stubby, "general purpose" beaks for gathering small seeds and insects; the long, needle-like beak of the hummingbird is just the right shape for inserting into narrow flowers, while the long, chisel-like beak of the woodpecker is ideal for drilling wood and chipping away bark. The flamingo has a boomerang-shaped beak that it uses as both a scoop and a sieve while it forages through shallow lakes and lagoons, filtering out all impurities from a mouthful of water and leaving only the microorganisms. Turnstones creep over rocky shores using their short anvil-shaped bill to hunt food under pebbles. The name of the spoonbill gives away the shape of its beak, which it moves rapidly from side to side while advancing through the shallows, snapping shut on any crustaceans or small fish along the way. As a group, shorebirds have developed the most extraordinary range of beaks so as to avoid competition with one another for the food available in the often narrow or limited feeding areas on coastlines, mudflats and estuaries. A long-billed shorebird and a short-billed species will both eat insect larvae but, as they are working at different depths, they each get what they want without depriving the other. Shorebirds with long beaks often have long legs, enabling them to wade and probe at the same time, and avoid competition with their shorter-billed chums back at the water's edge.

> A wonderful bird is the pelican,
> His bill can hold more than his belican,
> He can take in his beak,
> Food enough for a week,
> But I'm damned if I see how the helican.

**POET AND HUMORIST DIXON LANIER MERRIT
(1879–1954)**

The Australian pelican has the longest beak of all birds, measuring up to 18 inches, but the longest beak in relation to body length is that of the sword-billed hummingbird of South America. At 2 inches, the beak is longer than the body and the bird has to groom itself with its feet.

Why does the puffin have such a charming beak?

The puffin's colorful, triangular beak has caught the imagination of people for centuries; if evolution were ever to replace it with something more drab and functional it's unlikely the bird would get a second glance, let alone have a famous publishing imprint named after it. Resembling a cross between a parrot and a penguin, the puffin is sometimes affectionately referred to as "the clown of the sea," but the large red, yellow and blue beak, protruding from between its doleful eyes, has not been stuck at the top of its plump black and white body just so that humans can sit around sighing with pleasure at the sight of it. It is there for a serious purpose. Just as other birds sport more colorful plumage to attract a mate, so the puffin grows a colorful beak. In most birds it is the males alone who turn on the color in the breeding season, but with the puffins it is both sexes. The orange of the birds' feet also becomes brighter in the breeding season, while the beak grows a little bit longer each year. The size and color of the beaks are key factors by which the birds assess the fitness of potential partners.

The beaks are also highly efficient fishing tools, featuring backward-pointing spikes that enable them to gather dozens of small fish in one trip. Some seabirds swallow their catch and then regurgitate it for their chicks, but the puffin stacks the fish crosswise in its mouth, allowing it to save energy by taking one long foraging trip.

Once the breeding season is over, the colorful outer cases of the beak fall away to reveal an altogether duller object.

Where do birds sleep?

While owls, nightjars and other nocturnal birds head out into the gloom for a late evening meal, the rest of the bird world retires to sleep after another long, exhausting day foraging for food and dodging the cat. Most birds head to a roosting site where they will be safe from predators and protected from the elements. The body temperature of most species will drop by about a fifth to conserve energy and many species huddle together at night, especially in winter, to keep warm. Birds effectively spend the night in a state of hypothermia. Evolution having endowed them with the ability to maintain their balance and grip while they snooze, most songbirds will spend the night perched on a branch with their heads turned round and their beaks buried in their plumage. The way birds sleep varies between species and there is still much scientists don't know about avian sleep patterns. Many sleep in very short bursts to keep alert for predators while others have developed the ability to sleep with one eye open. Swifts and swallows sleep on the wing for a few seconds at a time high up in the sky, while the wandering albatross, a bird that flies all the way round the lower half of the world in a single journey in search of food, sleeps as it soars above the icebergs below. Ducks and other aquatic birds will sleep on land but many choose to spend the night on the water to avoid predators. Ducks sleep in a line with two on the ends keeping an eye open for intruders.

from **The Owl Against Robin**

Frowning, the owl in the oak complained him
Sore, that the song of the robin restrained him
Wrongly of slumber, rudely of rest.
"From the north, from the east, from the south and the west,
Woodland, wheat-field, corn-field, clover,
Over and over and over and over,
Five o'clock, ten o'clock, twelve, or seven,
Nothing but robin-songs heard under heaven:
How can we sleep?"

POET SIDNEY LANIER (1842–81)

Why is bird poo white?

In a roundabout way, like so many answers to questions about birds, it's all to do with flying. The science of this subject doesn't yield its explanation easily, but bear with me – imagine how people around the table will gasp when you clear your throat and announce: "I know why bird poop is white . . ."

With the exception of vultures and some storks, birds don't urinate because, as creatures that live and die by their ability to fly efficiently, they cannot afford to be weighed down by excess moisture. If a bird did urinate, it would have to consume such massive quantities of water it would spend most of its day drinking. But birds must still expel the potentially fatal toxins, including ammonia, which form when their food is broken down in the digestive system and its nitrogen content makes new compounds. Mammals get rid of nitrogen via their urine by making a less toxic yellow compound called urea, which needs a lot of water to flush it through. Hence urine is mainly water. On average mammals lose 30 times more water in expelling nitrogen waste than birds do. Birds get rid of their nitrogen by transforming it into a toxic compound called uric acid, made of tiny *white* crystals, which cannot be urinated away because it is not water-soluble like urea. The bird's incredibly efficient digestive system absorbs almost every last drop of water that passes through the body, allowing it to go comparatively long periods without a drink as well as survive in some of the world's most arid and unforgiving climates.

Why don't ducks mind getting wet?

Water really does just slide off a duck's back, as it does with most aquatic birds like swans, grebes and coots – and to a slightly lesser extent with nearly all birds. The plumage of a duck works in the same way as an oiled waterproof coat. Using its beak, the duck takes the waxy substance from a preening gland beneath its tail and wipes it over its body. Thousands of downy feathers under the plumage help to trap the air and preserve body temperature in cold water. Sometimes this can make a bird that dives for its food too buoyant, so it will dive down to expel the trapped air.

Cormorants and shags are the only water-based birds that don't have waterproof plumage. It is thought that this may help them dive more quickly to catch their prey since their sodden feathers do not retain air bubbles. After fishing, cormorants go ashore and hold out their wings to dry in the sun.

Why don't birds have penises?

There are a number of sensible reasons why evolution has shunned the penis option for most birds. Evolution has done everything in its gift to adapt birds for efficient flight. A bird must fly light so a penis – complete with compulsory external testicles – would be unwelcome excess baggage for nature's aviators. (Male birds do have gonads, buried deep inside the body, but they are tiny outside the breeding season.) Evolution has also worked out that it would be a poorly designed bird indeed that carried vulnerable dangly bits on its underside as it swooped in and out of bushes so many hundreds of times a day. Nor would it be a great idea for birds to mate by coupling together for more than a few seconds, what with so many sharp-clawed predators about. Birds need to escape in an instant and that's not so easy if they're lying on the lawn, locked in heavenly transport, making the bird with two backs. So both males and females have ended up with the cloaca and copulation lasts no longer than the shake of a tail.

Plain tasteless

Birds have a very poor sense of taste. It varies slightly from species to species but on average they have about 50 taste buds, compared to 9,000 in humans. Without teeth, birds swallow their food whole, leaving it to their powerful stomachs to break down the food.

A handful of birds including ducks, geese, ostriches and flamingos do have penises. The duck has one because it mates on water and the female is half-submerged during copulation. If it mated like other birds, with male and female touching cloacas, the droplet containing the sperm would be washed away, so a drake needs a penis to make sure the sperm is delivered safely.

The male Argentine lake duck has the longest penis of all vertebrates, measuring a whopping 16.7 inches, roughly the same length as the bird itself. (Other male ducks have to take consolation from the fact that the lake duck has the brains and personality of a dead fish, a really irritating quack and unattractive plumage.) In all ducks, the penis, like the female's vagina, is shaped like a corkscrew. The unusual shape of the penis allows the duck to keep it wound up inside until he needs it.

Tongue-tied woodpeckers

At 4 inches, the tongue of the woodpecker is four times longer than its beak and has to be curled round inside beneath the skin when it's not being used. The sticky tongue, which has sharp barbs on the end, is used for extracting the ants from deep in their nest. Ants are a staple part of the green woodpecker's diet: it will eat as many as 2,000 in a day and travel many miles to find them.

Sac de merde

Many birds, especially the smaller, defenseless ones, hide their nests to avoid their young being taken by predators and they go to great lengths to make sure they don't leave a trail of evidence to alert attackers to their whereabouts. Dumping excreta all over surrounding branches and leaves would be an obvious giveaway and so many chicks have developed the neat trick of shitting into a little internal sac. The parent pecks the chick on the butt and out comes a little white bag of feces, which the parent proceeds to swallow. When the chick grows older and its feces are less digestible, the parents carry the shit-sac from the nest and dump it at a safe distance. Just as humans do with diapers.

This season's fashion

When they molt, most birds lose a few feathers at a time, replacing the whole plumage over the course of one or two months, so as not to undermine their flying efficiency or insulation. For the majority of birds the molt comes at the end of the breeding season when their feathers are in a tattered state after months of hectic activity. Molting also uses up a lot of energy so late summer and early autumn is the best time of year because it is the least stressful and exhausting. The chicks have fledged and are out there fending for themselves, there is plenty of food around, it's not too cold and there is still thick foliage in which the more vulnerable birds can spend much of the day hidden from predators.

Most adult birds molt only once a year, but the current year's hatch will often renew their feathers three times before donning their adult plumage the spring after they were born. Though a few wait till afterwards, the majority of migratory birds molt shortly before they set off so that their feathers are in top aerodynamic condition for the long journey ahead. Some species molt twice a year, adopting a more colorful appearance in the breeding season. Birds of prey, which need to stay airborne to survive by hunting, molt in a constant process throughout the year.

Ducks do it naked

Unlike most other birds, ducks, geese and swans lose all their flight feathers at once, rendering them flightless for a period. They hide in reeds and rushes until new feathers grow, often congregating in a remote place in large numbers for safety reasons. If attacked by a predator their chances of survival are greater in a group than if they were alone. The male duck sheds the brightly colored plumage it wore for courting its partner, donning dull brown feathers, known as "eclipse" plumage, that make it virtually indistinguishable from the female for a few months.

Why are flamingos pink?

The stunning pink plumage of the flamingo is caused by the beta-carotene in its diet of shrimp and blue-green algae, which are both rich in the pigment. When deprived of these food sources in zoos, the flamingo turns white unless it is fed other foods rich in beta-carotene such as carrots, beets and sweet red peppers. (Salmon is pink because its diet includes crustaceans that contain the carotene.) You, too, can turn flamingo pink if you wish – if you're prepared to eat beets for breakfast, lunch and dinner for a few weeks!

Bird body facts

- The four toes of passerines, or songbirds, are designed and arranged for perching, with three pointing forward and one pointing back.

- No bird has teeth. Evolution has disposed of them to lighten the load and improve flying efficiency.

- All birds have tongues.

- Birds don't sweat. To lose heat, they pant and head for shade.

- As a general rule, the bigger the bird, the less it eats. Birds of prey eat a quarter of their weight every day, songbirds about half, while tiny hummingbirds consume twice their body mass in energy-boosting nectar.

Necking drinks

Most birds can't suck so they drink by taking a beak of water and then tipping back their heads. Only a handful of birds, including pigeons and doves, are able to use their tongues to consume water without having to tilt their necks.

A sight better

Sight is a bird's best sense. Its hearing is good as well – exceptional in most nocturnal species – but a bird lives or dies by the quality of its vision. A human being can lead a perfectly satisfactory life with poor eyesight, but a bird in need of glasses would perish very quickly. A bird's visual abilities are without equal in the animal kingdom, enabling it to carry out a wide range of crucial functions. Many birds fly at great speed through dense foliage and in dim light, and most have to be on the constant lookout for predators. A bird needs to locate food quickly and accurately. In the never-ending desperate quest for the energy it needs to maintain its highly demanding metabolism, it cannot afford to waste time flitting about the shrubbery sampling different insects and plants, mistaking grit for seed or, worse still, poisoning itself by wrongly identifying a specimen. Nor can it risk making itself vulnerable to predator attack by alighting on the ground or a branch for more than a few seconds. A female also needs to be able to assess the fitness of a potential partner by a close inspection of minute, telltale physical characteristics such as the color quality of the suitor's plumage. It's unhelpful, though, to make generalizations about avian vision because there are wide variations between orders of birds. Comparisons with other creatures are not that useful either because the way in which birds see is different.

Birds who have what their names suggest
Redwing
Crossbill
Blackcap
Spoonbill
Goldeneye
Goldcrest
Whitethroat
Razorbill
Pintail

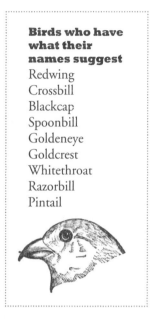

Eyes like tea saucers

If our eyes were in the same proportion to our heads as those of birds, we'd all be looking at the world through facial features the size of tea saucers and tennis balls. Apart from making it extremely difficult for anyone to take anyone else remotely seriously ever again, it would also mean that our brains would have to shrink in order to accommodate our massive eyeballs. Birds have the largest eyes relative to body size of all terrestrial vertebrates and their brains are among the smallest. The skull of a mammal is filled up mainly with brain, but in birds it is the eye that takes up most room. Some hawks and owls have eyes as large as human eyes, even though in overall body size they are between 120 and 150 times smaller. At 2 inches in diameter, the eye of the ostrich is the largest of any land animal. In some owls, the eyes make up over 30 percent of the weight of the head whereas in humans it is only about 1 percent – even though humans have exceptionally efficient sight as well.

It's all a bit of a blur for the scientists

Unable to sit birds down in front of an optician's letter chart and ask them to squawk what they see, scientists still have a great deal they don't know about the quality of avian vision. It is clear, though, even to the layman, that there is a great deal of discrepancy between the species. A domesticated chicken, one of the easier birds to test, has poor eyesight for the simple reason that there is no evolutionary pressure for it to see well. Unlike most birds, the chicken doesn't fly in and out of dense foliage as songbirds do, and it doesn't have to look very hard for its food as almost all wild birds do. More often than not, its food is right under its beak, placed there by a human being with dark plans to roast it or scramble its eggs.

Songbirds and birds of prey are thought to be able to focus on objects two or three times further away than humans can, with no more than a quick glance. In the retina of an animal eye there are thousands of receptor cells, and the more cells it has the sharper the images it sees. The human eye has about 200,000 cones per square millimeter, while the songbirds in your garden have roughly double that. Birds of prey, hovering and soaring to spot small mammals often hundreds of feet below, have four to six times as many as humans. The speed with which birds process information from visual sources may also be a factor. It is thought that many orders and species are able to understand what they are looking at with the merest glance whereas it may take humans and other mammals much longer.

Night goggles

A barn owl can spot prey in light so poor that were humans endowed with the equivalent ability we would be able to pick out an object by the light of a match over a mile away.

Why do some birds have eyes on the side of their heads and others on the front?

Most birds have eyes on the side rather than the front of their heads because it gives them better panoramic vision to help spot predators and food sources. When you see a thrush hopping about on the lawn with its head tilted to one side, it is looking for worms and not, as often thought, listening for them.

The woodcock has the best all-round vision: its eyes are positioned so far back in its head that it has a 360-degree view of its world without having to move its head.

But birds with good field of vision are unable to judge distance and perspective as well as creatures with binocular vision. Birds of prey, such as hawks, owls and eagles, are exceptions in the bird world in having eyes on the front of their heads, giving them the binocular or stereoscopic vision they need to see depth. A bird of prey needs to judge distance to exact measurements when diving and stooping at great speed to take its victim. To compensate for their smaller field of vision, birds of prey have developed the ability to rotate their heads all the way round.

Do birds see in color?

Birds' color vision is far more developed and sophisticated than ours. It enables them to spot prey at a distance and distinguish between good and bad sources of food, and allows females to make out minute differences in the quality of plumage when deciding which partner to take at the start of the breeding season. Like a woman being able to tell the color of a man's eyes or the cut of his suit from 100 paces, a female bird quickly works out the potential fitness of the suitor trying to impress her with his appearance. Scruffy, dull characters need not apply. Many birds – notably hummingbirds – have the ability to see ultraviolet light (shared with nectar-hunting insects), which helps them spy out their food sources of flowers and fruit. Owls, and other nocturnal birds, are exceptions to the general rule because good color vision would reduce the sensitivity of their sight in dim light.

No need to shout, I'm an owl

As most owls operate in the twilight hours of dawn and dusk – only a few species are strictly nocturnal – evolution has equipped them with a wide range of ingenious physical gifts and gadgets including superb camouflage, keen eyesight and a feather structure that allows them to swoop silently upon their prey. Above all, it is the astonishingly efficient if bizarre hearing system of the owl that sets it apart from its feathered colleagues; an owl can locate its prey by detecting the smallest rustle in the undergrowth. It has one ear set very marginally higher than the other and this asymmetry gives it the aural equivalent of binocular vision. The minuscule time difference between the sound being perceived in one ear and in the other provides a cross reference from which the owl can work out the exact location of its source.

The region of the brain that controls hearing is three to five times more developed in the owl than in most other birds and although its range of audible sounds is roughly the same as for humans its hearing is much more acute at certain frequencies.

The owl may be dozens of yards away sitting on a branch or gliding through the air but once it picks up the merest tremor of sound it will pinpoint its prey to within millimeters. If the animal moves, the owl's brain, moving faster than the most advanced GPS system, is able to make virtually instant recalculations as it swoops in for the kill. The owl has memorized every square inch of its terrain. Once the owl's hearing has locked on, the prey has no chance of survival even if it is buried under two feet of heavily impacted snow or thick brush.

The strictly nocturnal species, such as the barn owl, have the additional advantage of a round, hollowed-out face, which operates like a radar dish, collecting and channeling sounds into the ear openings. An owl's ears are positioned at the sides of its head, covered by the feathers of the facial disk. The pointy tufts sported by some species, such as the long-eared owl, are not ears at all but display feathers.

Taking the sting out of it

Bee-eaters need several hundred bees every day to feed their young and give themselves the extra energy required for the frenetic hunting in the breeding season. They take the sting out of bees by rubbing or whacking them to death on their perch.

Eiderdown . . . and almost out

Down feathers, the fluffy under-layer closest to the skin of ducks, geese and other aquatic birds, are among nature's best insulating materials. The warmest down comes from the eider duck, the UK's heaviest duck and the fastest through the air. It is a sea duck that spends much of its year inside the Arctic Circle and has developed its remarkable down in order to survive in freezing conditions. Eider down has been so sought after by man that by the end of the nineteenth century the bird was almost extinct. Its numbers have recovered but they are threatened once again – this time because the eider duck's dependence on coastal molluscs has brought it into conflict with mussel farmers.

Useless nostrils

Sight and hearing are the senses that a bird relies on for its survival. Birds have the equipment to smell, but the ability has been developed only in a tiny handful of the world's 10,000 species, most notably the kiwi. Many seabirds, too, including the shearwater, the fulmar and the storm petrel, Britain's smallest breeding seabird, have evolved with a very strong sense of smell to help them detect food sources at sea.

Most birds have two external, unobtrusive nostrils, or *nares*, located on the upper mandible of their beaks, which they use for breathing. Some diving species such as gannets, shags and cormorants don't have nostrils and breathe through the beak instead. Anyone who has jumped awkwardly into a swimming pool and felt a blast of water up their nose will understand why evolution has sealed up the nostrils of these birds.

Why don't penguins freeze to death when they molt?

Unlike most birds, that molt slowly, generally over a period of six to eight weeks, the penguin renews its feathers as quickly as possible. Most penguins take no more than two or three weeks to produce a fresh warm coat of feathers in a process known as a "catastrophic molt." They adopt this approach because even more than other birds they need to be waterproof and well insulated from the cold to maintain their aquatic lifestyle. A couple of weeks before the molt they start gorging food to put on as much weight as possible, almost doubling their body mass. During the molt they stay out of the water and live off their fat while their new feathers push out the old ones. The penguins huddle together to keep warm, rotating positions to make sure each does its turn on the freezing, wind-battered fringes of the group before returning to the relative heat of the center, which is roughly 50°F warmer than the edges.

Quite a stink

The long-running debate as to whether vultures locate carrion by sight or smell included a famous transatlantic feud in the early nineteenth century between the American artist and ornithologist John James Audubon and Charles "Squire" Waterton, an eccentric British naturalist and explorer who used to enjoy imitating a dog and biting the legs of his guests under the dinner table. The argument still hasn't been completely settled but what the experts know for sure is that the turkey vulture, a species found in the Americas, definitely forages for carrion by smell. All the others, including the African and Asian species, almost certainly use their sight, even if some can smell a little. From experiments carried out in the 1960s, we now know that the turkey vulture picks up the smell of mer-

> Birds are more colorful in the gentler light of early morning and late afternoon because the harsh glare of the midday sun makes their plumage appear paler.

captan, a gas produced by decaying flesh, and will be first on the scene as a result. Spotting its turkey vulture cousin tearing at the flesh, the larger black vulture will arrive and bully its way to the carcass, sticking its neck through the mouth and anus of the carcass to pull out its entrails. (Don't, whatever you do, try this at home. You'll never get the stains off your shirt collar.) The king vulture, yet bigger and more powerful, is next to reach the feast, and then it is the black vultures who must defer and step aside. And if there's a condor, one of the world's largest birds, in the vicinity, everyone else has to make way until the carcass has been torn wide open and the condor has eaten its fill.

Why does the toucan have such an enormous beak?

The giant, bright orange beak of the toucan, measuring more than half the length of the body in some cases, is what makes the bird one of the most instantly recognizable of the world's 10,000 species. But why it has such an extraordinary beak is a mystery the ornithologists have yet to crack. No theory holds water. The beak can't be a weapon because, in spite of its size and solid appearance, it is in fact incredibly lightweight, a honeycomb structure made from a fibrous protein called keratin, from which birds' feathers – and our fingernails – are also made. More feather duster than knuckle duster if it came to a fight. Its lightness explains how a toucan can apparently defy gravity when perched on a branch. The casual onlooker would think it only a matter of time before the weight of its huge orange mandibles sent the bird crashing to the ground or swinging upside down like a big bat, but the gargantuan beak actually makes up less than one twentieth of the toucan's entire body mass.

The beak may come in handy for plucking fruits on branches far away from those strong enough to support the bird's weight, but the experts are not convinced that this is the one and only reason that evolution would go to such lengths to produce, well, such a length. Nor does the beak appear to have been adapted for a particular style of eating or hunting. Toucans are not specialist feeders. They consume a lot of fruit and berries, but most species will also eat seeds, insects and even snakes, frogs, small mammals and the eggs of other birds. You don't need a beak the size of Cuba to eat any of the above, as many other bird species demonstrate. Nor do scientists believe that the beaks play a part in attracting a mate during the breeding season.

Although the birds will use their beaks to toss each other fruit, especially when they're feeling flirtatious and playful in the breeding season, evolution will not have spent millions of years developing this frankly ridiculous and mildly unsettling feature just so the birds can have a good old food fight. But at a stage in our civilization when scientists appear to know virtually everything there is to know about the natural world in which we live, isn't it wonderful that they still can't solve the mystery of the toucan's beak?

A Complex Relationship

BIRDS AND MAN

George V of England had a pink-gray pet parrot called Charlotte that he kept in his study at Sandringham and carried around with him, perched on his fingers or shoulder. Queen Mary was not amused by his habit of letting Charlotte wander across the breakfast table, unloading droppings among the marmalade pots and devilled kidneys. When the King took to his study to examine the latest batch of state documents, Charlotte sat on his shoulder, squawking loudly: "Well, what about it?"

~~~~~~~~~~~

I realized that if I had to choose, I would rather have birds than airplanes.

AVIATOR CHARLES LINDBERGH
(1902–74)

~~~~~~~~~~~

"" Among those I know of are a Prime Minister, a President, three Secretaries of State, a charwoman, two policemen, two Kings, two Royal Dukes, one Prince, one Princess, a Communist, seven Labour, one Liberal, six Conservative Members of Parliament, several farm-labourers earning ninety shillings a week, a rich man who earns two or three times more than that every hour of the day, at least forty-six schoolmasters, an engine-driver, a postman, and an upholsterer. ""

BRITISH ORNITHOLOGIST, NATURALIST, BROADCASTER AND AUTHOR JAMES FISHER (1912–70), WRITING ABOUT THE BIRD LOVERS HE KNEW *IN WATCHING BIRDS*

Why do some people hate cormorants?

If ever you are in any doubt about the evolutionary link between birds and dinosaurs, then take a look at the cormorant. Its long neck, sinister beady eyes and jet black plumage give it an arrestingly prehistoric appearance, more a reptile with feathers than a bird. Strangely for an

~~~~~~~~~

God loved the birds and invented trees. Man loved the birds and invented cages.

FRENCH PLAYWRIGHT JACQUES DEVAL (1890–1972), *AFIN DE VIVRE BEL ET BIEN*

~~~~~~~~~

aquatic bird, along with its close relative the shag, it has no oil-producing preening gland to water-proof its coat, which you'd think was some-thing of a design flaw given that the cormorant spends half its day diving underwater in search of fish. The reason is that, for a diver, buoyancy is no advantage; wet plumage helps it descend faster underwater to catch its prey. Conse-quently, the cormorant spends much of the rest of the day sitting on a rock, holding its wings out to dry in the wind in a pose that only adds to its dinosaur/pterodactyl image.

But it's not its slightly creepy silhouette so much as its invasion of inland waterways that upsets people, most especially fishermen who've been getting their wading pants in a terrible twist over the birds. To them the cormorants are "the black plague" robbing precious fish from our rivers, lakes, fisheries and reservoirs. In the United States, the double-crested cormorant causes the anxiety; in Britain, it is its close relative the great cormorant. All cormorants are highly efficient at catching fish – so good that the Chinese and Japanese have even trained them to do it for them – and fishermen believe that they are exhausting precious stocks, including the young fish. The truth, however, is that there is no hard evidence that cor-morants are actually causing more than minor damage. Fish have far more serious pressures, what with pollution, disease, degradation of their habitat – and fishermen! – as well as weird, changing weather pat-terns undermining their own food sources. The arrival of a few cormorants is the least of a fish's worries.

Slaughtered for hats

Tens of millions of birds were killed in the late 1800s and early twentieth century as shotgun-wielding hunters ravaged habitats around the globe to fill sacks of feathers for the booming plume industry. Ornamental feathers, worn in spectacular hat displays, were the height of fashion for the women of burgeoning middle classes on both sides of the Atlantic at the time. Eighty-five thousand people were employed in the US feather trade while there were a staggering 10,000 in the French capital, Paris.

Egrets and other herons, albatross and terns were the worst affected, with some species pushed to the brink of extinction before governmental action was taken to halt the slaughter. Dozens of species of small songbirds and birds of prey were hunted, too. During one walk through Manhattan in 1886, the celebrated American ornithologist Frank Chapman spotted 40 native species of birds on the hats of the women he passed. Hunters tended to kill adult birds, as they had bigger and better feathers, condemning the chicks to die back in the nest.

The feathers of many birds killed in the United States – a great number of them in the Florida Everglades – ended up on the heads of Europe's wealthier women. The records of one London trading house show that more than one million heron and egret skins were sold in the British capital between 1897 and 1911. In 1902 alone, almost 200,000 great egrets were killed to produce the 300 pounds of feathers sold through the London Commercial Sales Room. In 1911, the feathers of 129,000 egrets; 13,598 herons; 20,698 birds of paradise; 41,090 hummingbirds; 9,464 eagles, condors and other birds of prey and 9,472 other birds were sold at auction in London.

The Audubon Society in the United States and the Royal Society for the Protection of Birds (RSPB) in Britain, the world's first major conservation organizations, both came into existence during this time, each born out of the anger of campaigners appalled by the massacre. The introduction of federal laws, starting with the Lacey Act in 1900, triggered radical changes in the hunting of all American birds and by the outbreak of World War I, the guns of the plume trade hunters had fallen silent.

Learning lost languages parrot-fashion

During his journey in 1804 to track the source of the Orinoco River in modern-day Venezuela, the celebrated Prussian explorer and naturalist Alexander von Humboldt was introduced to some parrots that spoke words and phrases in a dialect that could not be identified by anyone in his traveling party. He was informed by his Carib Indian hosts that the bird had belonged to the neighboring Maypure tribe, which they had recently annihilated in a bloody battle. The parrot, in effect, was the last surviving speaker of the Maypure language. Von Humboldt made a phonetic recording of their speech and brought the transcript back to Europe. In 2000, American artist Rachel Berwick revived the dead language by teaching two parrots to speak the lost dialect and put them on display in an exhibition in London.

Why are parrots happy to sit in a cage when most other birds would go mad and die?

Parrots and other pet birds have been bred in captivity and they know no other life. Most wild birds would die in a small cage and the ones that spend almost their entire lives on the wing, like swallows, would die very quickly. Birds would survive in a large outdoor cage that replicates their wild habitat. You don't see many of these in people's gardens, however, for the simple reason that it is illegal to take birds or their eggs from the wild.

Gross domestic product

The economy of the tiny Pacific island of Nauru, a former British colony, was for the entire twentieth century based on the export of ancient bird droppings, making its inhabitants among the richest in the world. Three-quarters of the island was mined for the rock phosphate made from guano, and its extraction has left hundreds of cone-shaped limestone outcrops that give the landscape a haunting, outer-space appearance. Now that its once fertile land is exhausted of its rich deposits Nauru has become virtually uninhabitable, leaving the remaining islanders in a state of poverty.

~~~~~~~~~
I have been guilty of a great mistake. I have wasted my life with mineralogy which has led to nothing . . . Had I devoted myself to birds, their life and plumage, I might have produced something worth doing.

ENGLISH AUTHOR, ARTIST AND CRITIC JOHN RUSKIN (1819–1900)

~~~~~~~~

The Gettysburg Vultures

Every year hundreds of black vultures and turkey vultures congregate in the Pennsylvania skies above the site of the Battle of Gettysburg. They first appeared on July 1, 1863, the first of three days of intense fighting between Union and Confederate armies in the Civil War. Each side suffered roughly 20,000 casualties, among the highest of the four-year conflict, and the battlefield was also littered with the bodies of tens of thousands of dead horses, a feast of carrion for the vultures. There was so much food to be had that the birds are said to have stayed the winter and scavenged on the frozen carcasses. Every twelve months since then, for almost 150 years, they have been returning to the same spot. It is a chilling, haunting reminder of one of the United States' bloodiest days.

❝ Anytime you hear a man called "loony" just remember that's a great compliment to the man and a great disrespect to the loon. A loon doesn't wage war, his government is perfect being non-existent. He is the world's best fisherman and completely in control of his senses, thank you. ❞

JEROME LAWRENCE AND ROBERT E. LEE,
THE NIGHT THOREAU SPENT IN JAIL

Bird omens and superstitions

- A bird in the house is a presage of death or dire ill fortune.

- Two blackbirds together is a good omen. You will be blessed with good luck for a whole year if a blackbird nests in your house.

- The number of notes a cuckoo sings tells the listener how many years he or she has left to live.

- When a swallow stays close to its nest, bad weather is on the way.

- Your house will be protected from lightning if swallows nest under its eaves.

- Ill fortune befalls anyone who harms a wren or its nest.

- The blind will eventually regain their sight if they feed ravens.

- A dove is thought to bring good luck to a marriage. Doves are associated with peace and love as they often mate for life and both partners care for the upbringing of their young.

- The dove is the only bird whose form the devil can't assume.

- It was once thought that gulls and albatrosses carried the souls of dead sailors.

- Many people used to believe that the magpie was the devil in disguise. To dispel the ill fortune he would bring, on encountering the first magpie of the day, you were meant to tilt your hat, cross your fingers and say, "Good morning, Mr. Magpie."

- You are doomed if an owl calls your name, which is damned bad luck if you happen to be called Too-wit-too-woo, or Hoot.

Why do some people start cursing and waving sticks around at the sight of a flock of geese coming in to land?

Canada geese can destroy a lawn or a stretch of park in a couple of hours. Each bird is able to strip out over 100 blades of grass a minute, and will continue to do so, even into the night if there is a bright moon and a clear sky, until (a) it gets too dark, (b) there is no grass left or (c) an angry person with a stick catches up with them. They need to eat material that is readily available and easy to digest, and they need to eat it fast. While they are busy reducing the lawn to an expanse of mud, they add insult to injury by shitting almost as quickly as they eat. Geese have a very basic approach to food and digestion: get it down quick, shit it out quick, then move on to the next lawn.

Forget Viagra, eat a sparrow

There have been a host of theories put forward to explain the mystery of why the sparrow has been disappearing from our city centers, but perhaps the most outlandish is the one that claims the little birds have all been captured and cooked by sex maniacs who believe that the meat is an aphrodisiac. The sparrow has been associated with lust from Classical times and in the seventeenth century Nicholas Culpeper, a highly influential physician and botanist, wrote without so much as a hint of irony: "This is an undeniable aphorism that whatsoever a creature is addicted unto, they move or incite the man or the woman, that eats them, to the like: and therefore partridges, quails, sparrows, etc. being extremely addicted to venery, they work the same effect in those men and women that eat them . . . the brain of sparrows when eaten provokes the lust exceedingly."

Do geese mind being force-fed to make foie gras?

It depends on who you talk to. Put this question to a French restaurant owner or one of the 30,000 people working in France's foie gras industry and you'll probably receive one of the following answers, allowing for some losses in translation:

a. Non! Ça ne pose pas de problèmes aux oiseaux.
b. Oui, un petit peu but who cares? It's extremely delicious.
c. Why don't you leave me alone and go and see the chicken farmer next door if you want to see real bird cruelty?
d. Pardon, je ne comprends pas. Au revoir, Monsieur Rosbif.

Foie gras, French for "fat liver," is a highly prized and expensive delicacy made from the enlarged liver of a duck or goose. Opponents of its production contend that the force-feeding of large quantities of grain, a process known as *gavage*, causes severe distress to the birds. For the animal rights activist, *gavage* is as cruel as veal production and the fur trade. A foie gras duck or goose is bred specially for the purpose and kept in a small cage so that it can't turn round. When the bird is about two months old, it is force-fed several pounds of fat-soaked cornmeal two or three times a day through a long metal tube inserted deep

**Top five egg-
producing states**

1. Iowa
2. Ohio
3. Indiana
4. Pennsylvania
5. California

into its throat. When the liver has expanded many times beyond its natural size, the bird is slaughtered. (Being migratory birds, ducks and geese have a great capacity for putting on weight. In the wild they pile on the pounds to provide them with the energy reserves they need to fly thousands of miles.) The producers say that as ducks and geese don't have a gag reflex and swallow their food whole, *gavage* doesn't bother them. Animal rights activists claim that the birds are not so relaxed about their eccentric feeding arrangements, producing reports of esophageal wounds, ruptured livers, general ill-health, painful deaths and so forth, to justify their protests.

Foie gras producers counter that even if the claims were true, their opponents would do the cause of animal welfare far more good if they turned their attention to the world's poultry industry, which is responsible for hundreds of millions of animal deaths each year and an immeasurable amount of cruelty to the chickens living in barbaric factory farms. Besides, they say, what business is it of a government or a lobby group to tell people what they should or should not eat?

Bird Watcher

In Wall Street once a potent power,
And now a multi-millionaire
Alone within a shady bower
In clothes his valet would not wear,
He watches bird wings bright the air.

The man who mighty mergers planned,
And oil and coal kinglike controlled,
With field-glasses in failing hand
Spies downy nestlings five days old,
With joy he could not buy for gold.

Aye, even childlike is his glee;
But how he crisps with hate and dread
And shakes a clawlike fist to see
A kestrel hover overhead:
Though he would never shoot it dead.

Although his cook afar doth forage
For food to woo his appetite,
The old man lives on milk and porridge
And now it is his last delight
At eve if one lone linnet lingers
To pick crushed almonds from his fingers.

BRITISH POET ROBERT SERVICE (1874–1958)

Chairman Mao's Great Sparrow Campaign

Sparrows, en masse, can be a nuisance to farmers, munching their way through fields of ripening grain and breaking the stalks when they perch on them. They tend to operate from the safety of a boundary hedge, which is why you may have seen a 10-foot-wide band round the edge of a crop field that has been stripped bare. In 1958 China's Chairman Mao Zedong, leader of the Communist Revolution, who had figured out that each bird eats 11 pounds of grain every year, tried to exterminate all his country's sparrows in what was called the Great Sparrow Campaign. This was part of his Four Pests Campaign, an ambitious – some would say utterly insane – plan to rid China of all rats, mosquitoes, flies and sparrows. For the sparrow project, the army roamed the countryside firing shots into the air, while peasants were ordered to leave their homes and bang some pots and pans in a bid to kill the birds by exhausting them. Millions of birds died and thousands of nests were destroyed, but when the harvest yield then went down still further, people realized that the sparrows were needed to keep down the insects eating the crops. Sparrow numbers soon recovered. One–nothing nature.

English poet and painter William Blake on birds

A robin redbreast in a cage
Puts all heaven in a rage.

He who shall hurt the little wren
Shall never be belov'd by men.

When thou seest an eagle, thou seest a portion of genius;
lift up thy head!

The Owl and the Nightingale

Florence Nightingale saved a baby owl from some boys who were tormenting it at the Parthenon in Athens where she had stopped off on her return from Egypt in 1850. The "Lady with the Lamp" christened the owl Athena, smuggled it aboard her ship and took it back to England where it became something of an attraction in the Nightingale household, perching on Florence's fingers to feed and happily sitting in her pocket as she went about her daily business. When Nightingale came back from the Crimea in 1856, after tending to the injured soldiers of the British Army, her family rushed to greet her in London, leaving Athena in the attic of the family home. When the gathering returned, they hurried upstairs to see Athena, only to find her lying on her back, claws in the air, dead as a dodo. Florence, so stoical in her military field hospitals, burst into tears on the spot. The bird was stuffed and can be seen today in the Florence Nightingale Museum at St. Thomas's Hospital in London.

She was not quite what you would call refined. She was not quite what you would call unrefined. She was the kind of person that keeps a parrot.

MARK TWAIN (1835–1910)

For those who practise it, bird-watching is not only a sport and a science, but also something near a religion, and after all its externals have been inventoried the essence stays incommunicable.

BRITISH ORNITHOLOGIST AND ENVIRONMENTALIST
MAX NICHOLSON, WHO FOUNDED THE BRITISH TRUST FOR
ORNITHOLOGY (BTO) IN 1938

One for sorrow
Two for joy
Three for a wedding
Four for a boy
Five for silver
Six for gold
Seven for a secret never to be told
Eight for heaven
Nine for hell
And ten for the devil's own self.

VERSION OF TRADITIONAL RHYME ABOUT SEEING MAGPIES (ALSO SAID OF CROWS, THE MAGPIES' COUSINS)

Birds as bombs

Genghis Khan used birds as incendiary bombs when his Mongol hordes laid siege to the city of Volohoi in the early thirteenth century. Unable to breach the defences by more conventional means, the Mongol emperor tricked the inhabitants of the largely wooden city by offering peace in return for their gift of thousands of swallows and cats. His troops then fixed strips of burning cloth to the cats and birds and released them at the city's edge. Many of the flaming creatures fled back into the city, setting dozens of buildings on fire. In the pandemonium that followed, the Khan's army were able to breach the defences and overrun the city.

Why don't people eat crow?

"To eat crow" is an old expression with the same meaning as "to eat humble pie": to admit being wrong. But many people used to eat crow, because it was a perfectly acceptable alternative to fancier game meats. It was not a rich man's dish, but those who have tried it say it tastes a little like duck and the darkest meat of chicken. Rooks, starlings and dunlin (in coastal areas) were also eaten in rural households up until canned foods became widely available in the early twentieth century. Like most birds, crows have no white meat on them and, being scrawnier beasts than domestic fowl, with most of the meat on the breast, you will need several to make a meal. Cook the breasts as you would chicken. If one of the local guns ever offers you a couple of brace of *Corvus corone*, whip up the following simple recipe and impress your friends and family with your resourcefulness.

Pan-fried crow breast in breadcrumbs

Remove the breast meat from the carcasses and tenderize it with a meat mallet. Dunk the pieces in beaten egg and then into breadcrumbs or a spiced flour mixture. Fry them with some ham in hot oil, turning them over at least once. Connoisseurs say the middle should have a touch of pink.

And these are they which ye shall have in abomination among the fowls; they shall not be eaten, they are an abomination: the eagle, and the ossifrage, and the ospray, and the vulture, and the kite after his kind; every raven after his kind; and the owl, and the night hawk, and the cuckow, and the hawk after his kind, and the little owl, and the cormorant, and the great owl, and the swan, and the pelican, and the gier eagle, and the stork, the heron after her kind, and the lapwing, and the bat.

Leviticus 11:13–19

Bird phrases

Swan song

Pecking order

Ugly duckling

Give the bird

Birdbrain

Bird's nest

Stool pigeon

Sitting duck

Penguin suit

For the birds

Up with the lark

Chicken out

Spring chicken

Birds and the bees

Bird's-eye view

Lame duck

Hen party

Night owl

Cold turkey

Take under your wing

Ruffle someone's
feathers

Home bird

Rare bird

A dead duck

Cook somebody's goose

Have goose pimples

Wild goose chase

Waiter, I think someone's spat in my soup

The principal ingredient of the Chinese dish bird's nest soup is the saliva of a swiftlet, or cave swift, found in southern Asia and the islands of the Pacific. The swifts build their cup-shaped nests using saliva, which hardens when it dries. When dissolved in hot water the nests create a thick, gelatinous mixture, which is rich in nutrients and supposedly helpful in relieving a wide range of health problems – including asthma and poor digestion – and boosting the immune system and libido.

The nests were once harvested in the wild but today they are taken from concrete structures built specifically to attract flocks of the swifts. Bird's nest soup is a growing, highly lucrative industry serving restaurants in China, Hong Kong and New York where customers will pay up to $100 for a bowl.

" English Sparrows are being properly appreciated. Hundreds of them are now caught by enterprising people for sale to certain restaurants where reed birds are in demand. A German woman on Third Avenue has three traps set every day, and she catches probably seventy-five a week. They are cooked and served to her boarders the same as reed birds and are declared quite as great a delicacy. This German woman bastes them, leaving the little wooden skewer in the bird when served. They are cooked with a bit of bacon . . . The females are the choice meat. The males can be told by the circle of white feathers at the neck. The females are as plain as Quakeresses . . . Sparrow pie is a delicacy fit to set before a king. "

NEW YORK TIMES, JULY 20, 1887

GOLDEN RULES FOR FEEDING BIRDS

- Never feed salty foods to birds. A bird can't digest salt and it will damage its nervous system.

- Put out only the quantity that can be eaten in one day – or you risk attracting mice and rats.

- Make sure you provide birds with water as well. They need to drink (and wash).

- Be mindful of hygiene risk; wash your hands thoroughly after filling feeders and bird baths and wear gloves when you scrub them out. Let them dry before refilling to kill off harmful bacteria and prevent mold build-up.

- Place feeders and tables in positions safe from ambush by cats, and not too close to house windows. If birds don't like where you've put them, they simply won't come. Move the feeders around until the birds arrive.

- Wash out and fill up bird baths almost daily in summer.

- Keep tables and areas beneath feeders clear of droppings, which quickly become infected with hazardous bacteria and diseases.

Sparrow pie was a common dish in Britain until World War I, and songbirds such as the blackbird and the thrush have been a delicacy on mainland Europe for centuries. They were particularly popular in autumn after the birds had gorged themselves on ripened grapes. Dutch Customs officials made a number of spectacular finds in the 1990s, seizing shipments from China containing millions of plucked frozen sparrows, en route to Italy, highlighting that there is still great appetite for small wild birds.

Birds and the law

Most migratory birds (i.e., wild birds) found in the United States are protected by international treaties as well as US laws. No part of protected birds, live or dead, including feathers, claws, bones, skins, their eggs or nests, can be possessed without appropriate permits, which are almost impossible to obtain. It is lawful, however, to shoot some

STATE BIRDS OF THE UNITED STATES

American Goldfinch – Iowa, New Jersey, Washington

Baltimore Oriole – Maryland

Bluebird – Missouri, New York

Blue Hen Chicken – Delaware

Brown Thrasher – Georgia

Cactus Wren – Arizona

Common Gull – Utah

California Quail – California

Cardinal – Illinois, Indiana, Kentucky, North Carolina, Ohio, Virginia, West Virginia

Chickadee – Maine, Massachusetts

Common Loon – Minnesota

Eastern Brown Pelican – Louisiana

Great Carolina Wren – South Carolina

Hermit Thrush – Vermont

introduced birds, including European starlings, house sparrows and rock pigeons, which are considered agricultural pests. Some birds can also be killed in the hunting season, under strict federal and state laws.

Contrary to his depiction as a gentle character in the classic 1962 film that bears his name, the Birdman of Alcatraz was a violent bully loathed by his fellow inmates in the various prisons where he spent his entire adult life. Robert Stroud ran away from home at 13 and within five years he was working as a pimp in Alaska. He was jailed for 12 years after shooting dead an acquaintance who had beaten Gould's prostitute girlfriend. After stabbing a fellow prisoner, he was transferred to Leavenworth Prison in Kansas in 1912, where he began to educate himself through university extension courses, taking a particular interest in ornithology. In 1916, he took time off from his studies to stab and kill a guard. He was sentenced to hang, but following a plea

Lark Bunting – Colorado

Mockingbird – Arkansas, Florida, Mississippi, Tennessee, Texas

Mountain Bluebird – Idaho, Nevada

Nene – Hawaii

Purple Finch – New Hampshire

Ring-necked Pheasant – South Dakota

Rhode Island Red – Rhode Island

Roadrunner – New Mexico

Robin – Connecticut, Michigan, Wisconsin

Ruffed Grouse – Pennsylvania

Scissor-tailed Flycatcher – Oklahoma

Western Meadowlark – Kansas, Montana, North Dakota, Nebraska, Oregon, Wyoming

Willow Ptarmigan – Alaska

Yellowhammer – Alabama

from his mother, President Woodrow Wilson commuted his sentence to life imprisonment in solitary confinement. It was then, with no humans to befriend, shoot or stab, that he began raising and studying birds. Some of his research was smuggled out of prison and published in his book *Stroud's Digest on the Diseases of Birds* (1943), which became an important work of its time in its field. In 1942, he was transferred to Alcatraz, the prison island off San Francisco, where he was allowed to continue his studies but was barred from further publishing ventures. He died in 1963 with no friends or admirers, but there was nothing he couldn't tell you about avian pathology.

How the starlings conquered America

Africa's red-billed quelea is probably the world's most populous bird, but the starling comes in a close second. Today, the starling is a common sight in the United States where their numbers have grown exponentially since they were introduced from Europe at the end of the nineteenth century by Eugene Schieffelin, an eccentric millionaire drug manufacturer. Schieffelin wanted every songbird mentioned in the plays of William Shakespeare to be enjoyed by New Yorkers, but he was unsuccessful with attempts to introduce skylarks, chaffinches and song thrushes. The starling, however, is one of the world's hardiest, most adaptable birds and quickly found a niche for itself in the local ecology. Schieffelin released 100 of them in Central Park in 1890. Within a hundred years there were 250 million of them living in the United States.

The Canary Islands were named after the wild Mastiff-like dogs that lived there, and not for the birds of the same name, as is commonly supposed. The Romans gave Gran Canaria, the largest of this string of Atlantic islands, the name Canaria Insula, meaning Island of the Dogs.

A BEGINNER'S GUIDE TO BIRDWATCHING

- Get a good identification book. There are lots to choose from today.

- Buy a pair of binoculars (7x or 8x magnification are the best). There are perfectly good ones for under $75.

- Start in your garden or local park. If you know any experienced birdwatchers, try to spend a day with them to learn some tips.

- Buy a birdsong CD so you can start to learn the songs and calls of some of the most common species.

- Join a local birdwatching club.

- To see a variety of species seek out the best sites near to you, including woodland, meadows, estuaries, coastlines, riverbanks and lakes.

- Read up on the behavior of birds to learn where and at what time of the day or year you are most likely to see them.

- Buy an alarm clock. It's often just after daybreak when birds are at their most active, especially in the breeding season with so many extra mouths to feed.

- When you feel confident enough to leave your garden and start venturing further afield, wear dull, natural colors, or better still camouflage clothing, to blend in with your surroundings.

- Always find a bird with your naked eye first. It's no good searching with your binoculars because the field of vision is too narrow.

> The eggs of the turkey are almost as mild as those of the hen; the egg of the goose is large, but well-tasted. Duck's eggs have a rich flavour; the albumen is slightly transparent, or bluish, when set or coagulated by boiling, which requires less time than hen's eggs. Guinea-fowl eggs are smaller and more delicate than those of the hen. Eggs of wild fowl are generally coloured, often spotted; and the taste generally partakes somewhat of the flavour of the bird they belong to. Those of land birds that are eaten, as the plover, lapwing, ruff, &c., are in general much esteemed; but those of sea-fowl have, more or less, a strong fishy taste.

MRS. BEETON (1836–65)

Activists in a flap over battery hens

Until World War II, the majority of American eggs came from farm flocks of fewer than 400 hens, most of them living in free-range conditions. Today, most of the nation's 240 million laying birds exist in flocks of over 100,000, each laying around 250 eggs a year for an annual total of 75 billion. To the growing consternation of animal welfare campaigners, most laying hens in the United States, as elsewhere in the developed world, live in very cramped battery cages in industrial, intensive farming systems. A battery cage in the United States typically holds five hens, giving each bird less space than a piece of writing paper in which to live. (In Europe, the legal requirements are only marginally more generous.) The birds are unable to stand up to their full height, preen themselves or flap their wings as they would be able to do in their natural environment. Cages have a sloping wire mesh floor and are kept in rows stacked in tiers, like a giant avian apartment block with tens of thousands of residents. In most farms, the battery sheds are artificially lit and ventilated. The birds leave their cramped cages and experience natural light and fresh air for the first time when are taken away to be slaughtered. A recent report by Compassion Over Killing (COK), a Washington-based animal advocacy organization, highlighted the welfare issues of the nation's quarter billion egg-producing chicken hens, describing what happens when the birds have outlived their usefulness:

> After the second laying cycle, battery hens are gathered and transported to slaughter plants. At the plants, the hens are shackled by their legs and hung

upside-down on a long conveyer belt. Shackling often breaks the hens' fragile bones; by the time of slaughter, close to half of the birds have suffered broken bones. The hens are then submerged into an electrified water bath, which is supposed to render them unconscious, but many birds have their throats slit while fully conscious. Birds are not protected by the federal Humane Methods of Slaughter Act and are thus not required to be unconscious before being killed.

Under pressure from activists, the European Union has scheduled to phase out battery farms by 2012 and, COK, along with other US welfare organizations, have urged the US government to follow this example.

from **Home Thoughts, from Abroad**
And after April, when May follows,
And the whitethroat builds, and all the swallows!
Hark, where my blossom'd pear-tree in the hedge
Leans to the field and scatters on the clover
Blossoms and dewdrops – at the bent spray's edge –
That's the wise thrush; he sings each song twice over,
Lest you should think he never could recapture
The first fine careless rapture!
And though the fields look rough with hoary dew,
All will be gay when noontide wakes anew
The buttercups, the little children's dower
– Far brighter than this gaudy melon-flower!
ROBERT BROWNING (1812–89)

Pigeons: war heroes to zeroes

Today, an email message clicks into our inbox with a piece of important information; 100 years ago a pigeon fluttered back into its roost with the news tied to its body. As soon as man discovered that a pigeon had the ability to return to its nest from hundreds of miles away, he began to use the bird as a means of long-distance communication. We know pigeons were widely used by Greeks and Romans for a whole host of purposes, from passing back vital military information to sending personal letters and delivering the results of the Olympic Games. In the Middle Ages, the cities of the Middle East were all linked by an extensive network of pigeon post. At the turn of the twentieth century, English soccer fans smuggled birds into away soccer games and released them at half-time and the final whistle to fly home and inform the locals of the score. Pigeons played an important role in the two World Wars, saving thousands of lives in conflicts, carrying messages back from soldiers and undercover agents behind enemy lines. In World War I they often flew through heavy bombardment and poison gas to deliver vital information. The birds were also released from convoy ships in the Atlantic after a U-boat torpedo attack, giving the coordinates of the location of the sinking ship so that the crew might be rescued. Today, pigeons are no longer cherished and admired as they were for so many centuries. On the contrary, they are regarded as an unhygienic nuisance and millions of them are exterminated every year across the globe by pest controllers.

Goose-stepping army reaches London

For hundreds of years, until the late nineteenth century, huge flocks of geese, reared mainly in East Anglia, England, were marched to London markets after having their feet dipped in tar and sand to help them on their long journey. (Turkeys were fitted with little leather boots for their comfort.) The goose was a very important feature in households of the day, providing eggs and meat to eat, feathers for quills, pillows and cushions and fat for cooking as well as for use as a dry-skin cream and a cure for chest and throat complaints when mixed with honey. Today, goose feathers are still used in a wide variety of products, including bedding, natural toothpicks and badminton shuttlecocks.

No goose before or since has achieved such celebrity as a gander called Old Tom, whose death after 37 years of living in London's Leadenhall Market was reported at great length in the *London Times* on April 16, 1835. Old Tom had become a favorite among traders and customers alike in the market after he emerged a lone survivor from the slaughter of 34,000 geese. Following his death he was embalmed and lay in state, his body guarded by two other geese, and hundreds of Londoners flocked to pay their respects, each of them handing over a penny for the privilege. The money raised went toward a grave and headstone in Leadenhall Market, the inscription declaring Old Tom to be "The chief of geese, the poulterer's pride."

Eco-thieves target rare birds

The caged-bird trade is very good business for crooks and very bad news for nature lovers – not to mention the birds themselves. The sharp decline in many exotic bird species can be laid at the door of the smugglers. Roughly a third of the world's most endangered species are threatened by human interference and exploitation. The plundering of wild populations is concentrated mainly in the South American rain forest (what's left of it) and China, Indonesia and the

Philippines, but the birds, many of which die during capture or in transit, are sold in countries across the world, including Britain and the United States. Songbirds, such as finches, warblers and weavers, are hunted and traded, but their value is low and the big money comes from the more exotic, colorful birds of the parrot family such as macaws, Amazons, cockatoos, lovebirds, parakeets, mynahs and toucans. It is virtually impossible to obtain reliable figures from this nefarious, murky world, but conservative estimates suggest that roughly two million birds are sold every year.

Stork, stork, fly away,
Stand not on one leg, I pray,
See your wife is in her nest,
With her little ones at rest.
They will hang one,
And fry another;
They will shoot a third,
And roast his brother.
HANS CHRISTIAN ANDERSEN (1805–75)

❝ About one thing the Englishman has a particularly strict code. If a bird says *Cluk bik bik bik bik* and *caw* you may kill it, eat it, or ask Fortnums to pickle it in Napoleon brandy with wild strawberries. If it says *tweet* it is a dear and precious friend and you'd better lay off it if you want to remain a member of Boodles. ❞
ENGLISH WRITER AND BROADCASTER CLEMENT FREUD (1924–2009)

HOW TO HELP YOUR BIRDS IN WINTER

Winter is a difficult time of year for birds. The days are short, there is less time to feed and the nights are cold, which means they must eat a lot more food if they are to have the energy to keep warm and survive until the morning. As if that wasn't enough, food is harder for them to find in winter. Most insects are hibernating, worms are harder to extract from the colder earth, and snow and ice can make it even more difficult. Feeding birds the leftovers from your kitchen will help many of them to survive into spring, but be careful what you give them.

What to feed birds from your kitchen in winter:

- Cold boiled **potatoes** or roast potatoes, opened up.

- Cold cooked **root vegetables** such as carrots and parsnips.

- Cut-up **apples and pears** are gratefully received even if they're a little bruised. Dried fruits, such as currants and raisins, are popular too.

- Pieces of mild to medium strength **hard cheese** like cheddar are popular with many birds including robins, blackbirds and song thrushes. Wrens like it too but for them to take it you have to place it near the hedgerows where they skulk.

- **Fat** from cuts of unsalted meat can be laid out in large slices. Secure them to the ground or bird table with a heavy object to stop larger birds flying away with the entire piece.

- Old cake and broken **cookies** are a welcome treat, being high in fat.

Don't make the mistake of feeding salted foods as birds can't digest them and they may damage their nervous system. Don't provide soft fats such as polyunsaturated margarines and vegetable oils as these can destroy the waterproofing and insulating qualities of feathers.

The Majesty of Flight

HOW AND WHY BIRDS FLY

Happier of happy though I be like them
I cannot take possession of the sky,
Mount with a thoughtless impulse, and wheel there,
One of a mighty multitude whose way and motion is a harmony
    and dance
Magnificent.

ENGLISH POET WILLIAM WORDSWORTH (1770–1850)

Why did birds start to fly?

We don't know for sure but one theory is that birds' ancestors – dinosaurs that resembled running lizards – leaped higher and higher over a period of millions of years as they ran to catch insects, flapping their feathered arms for extra propulsion. This is called the "ground-up" theory. The more credible theory is that these ancient creatures had much in common with the flying squirrels and lizards alive today, climbing trees with their sharp-clawed hind feet and then gliding back down to the ground. That way the creature saved energy by not having to scuttle down one tree before running up another. It was then just a short evolutionary step, albeit one that went on for tens of millions of years, to start gliding from branch to branch, tree to tree; then on to the next stage of flying longer distances. This is known as the "Trees-down" hypothesis. As for why they might want to go up trees in the first place, much of the world was carpeted in forest way back in prehistory and creatures learned to climb trees for a number of reasons, including to lay eggs, to feed off insects and to escape predators.

Dawn
Ecstatic bird songs pound
the hollow vastness of the sky
with metallic clinkings –
beating color up into it
at a far edge,– beating it, beating it
with rising, triumphant ardor, –
stirring it into warmth,
quickening in it a spreading change, –
bursting wildly against it as
dividing the horizon, a heavy sun
lifts himself – is lifted –
bit by bit above the edge
of things, – runs free at last
out into the open – !lumbering
glorified in full release upward –
   songs cease.
POET WILLIAM CARLOS WILLIAMS (1883–1963)

The magic of flight

So accustomed are we to the sight of a bird in flight that we have ceased to be amazed by it, but how evolution has allowed an animal to achieve mastery of the air is one of the great marvels of nature. The bird's extraordinary body has been designed to minute specifications in order that it may rise above the rest of the animal world and live life on the wing. Humans couldn't have devised a better flying machine if they had spent tens of millions of years in the effort.

The bird has become by far the lightest animal in relation to its size in order that it may fly. (Flightless birds such as penguins and ostriches are very heavy because they no longer need to get airborne.) The bird doesn't have a heavy tail to drag around, nor any teeth, while its reproductive organs, male and female, shrink to virtual non-existence outside the breeding season. Bone-matter is heavy so evolution has got rid of as much of it as it can – over millions of years, of course – by eliminating some bones altogether, fusing others and hollowing out those that remain, filling them with air for added buoyancy.

In order to meet the enormous demands imposed by flying on the metabolism, a bird has the most efficient breathing system in the animal kingdom. It has a four-chambered heart, just as a human does, but proportionately the heart weighs six times more and its beat is incredibly rapid. The resting heart rate of a small garden bird is about 500 beats per minute while its respiratory system takes up 20 percent of its body volume compared with 5 percent in humans. A bird has a series of air sacs throughout its body (nine in most species) that are connected to its two lungs and its hollow bones.

The sacs in the back are called the "posterior" and those in the front of the body the "anterior" air sacs. Evolution has devised a highly resourceful system that passes the air in a one-way, staggered flow through the bird's lungs, providing a constant supply of fresh oxygen-rich air. When a bird inhales through the nostrils at the base of its beak, the air passes first into the posterior air sacs and then, when it breathes out, into the lungs. When the next breath is inhaled into the posterior sacs, the air from the first moves from the lungs into the anterior air sacs. When it exhales again, the air from the first breath is expelled from the bird, while the second breath travels into the lungs and so on . . .

The way a human breathes is not especially efficient but it's good enough to allow us to go about our daily business of clubbing each other, running away from woolly mammoths, playing football and so forth. We absorb just 20 percent of the oxygen from each breath whereas a bird absorbs 100 percent thanks to its network of air sacs.

As a finishing touch, the bird's streamlined plumage minimizes air resistance, improves aerodynamics and reduces the amount of energy needed to move through the air.

The birds that don't fly, or aren't very good at it, evolved from efficient flying ancestors to suit specific ecological niches.

Golden eagles often hunt in pairs. One flies over the contours of the land, flushing out alarmed prey, which, if all goes to plan, rears up straight into the talons of the second bird. Eagles are seriously impressive hunters with a host of techniques. They can spot a hare from over a mile away and plunge straight down from a great height to take it.

The Dalliance of the Eagles

Skirting the river road,
(my forenoon walk,
my rest,)
Skyward in air a
sudden muffled
sound, the dalliance
of the eagles,
The rushing amorous
contact high in space together,
The clinching interlocking claws, a living, fierce, gyrating wheel,
Four beating wings, two beaks, a swirling mass tight grappling,
In tumbling turning clustering loops, straight downward falling,
Till o'er the river pois'd, the twain yet one, a moment's lull,
A motionless still balance in the air, then parting, talons loosing,
Upward again on slow-firm pinions slanting, their separate diverse flight,
She hers, he his, pursuing.
POET WALT WHITMAN (1819–92)

Why do you never see a swift sitting down?

Like the hummingbird, another extraordinarily adept flier, the swift is virtually incapable of walking. It is the evolutionary price it has paid for its spectacular aerial skills. Both species of bird belong to the order known as Apodiformes, from the Greek meaning "footless." The swift is so bad at walking that it's more stable if it clings to a vertical surface than it is on level ground.

The swift is even more useless on terra firma than the virtually legless shearwater and will never land on the ground deliberately. If it is blown there in severe weather or collapses after an arduous migration, it struggles to get airborne again and is extremely vulnerable to predators. The only time the swift settles on solid matter is when, during the breeding season, it returns to the nest it has built from grass, feathers and spittle, either in a hole in a cliff or in the loft of a house. For the other nine or so months of the year, the swift is in the air. It eats in the air, mouth open like a basking shark, surviving entirely on a diet of insects; it drinks in the air, skimming the surface of a pond or a lake, and possibly by consuming raindrops too. The swift even mates on the wing, the male landing on the female's back for a couple of seconds. But the prize for the bird with the greatest number of continuous flying hours must surely go to the sooty tern, which remains airborne from the moment it has fledged until it starts breeding, a full six years later at the earliest.

The shearwater, meanwhile, is so adapted to the aquatic life that its legs have effectively become worthless stubs. They are positioned so far back on its body that it can barely stand up or walk, forcing it instead to shuffle along on its belly. This shortcoming makes it vulnerable to predators so it nests in a burrow in the ground and it comes ashore only at night.

Nature's fastest creatures

Flying is an incredibly efficient way of moving: a human sprinter can run the equivalent of between five and seven lengths of his own body per second; a cheetah, the fastest animal, can cover 16 to 18; but a bird can move at about 75 body lengths per second, making it as fast as a jet plane in relation to its size.

Why is it that millions of birds in huge swirling flocks never collide?

This question has fascinated scientists and bird-watchers for centuries, and it is only recently that they have gotten close to solving the mystery. Ornithologists call the mass simultaneous gyration of birds the "chorus-line effect." It used to be thought that a leader bird was somehow choreographing the show, perhaps by transmitting commands through some mysterious, extrasensory means that only birds could understand. But scientists have recently worked out that each bird takes its cue from the bird next to it and acts on it almost instantaneously,

just like the wave inside a stadium. As flocks grow in size, the speed of the twists and turns and wheeling increases, leading to the spectacular display we see when over a million starlings congregate at the end of the day before heading off to their communal roost. But we still don't know *why* they do it.

~~~~~~~~~~~~~~~~~~~~~~~~~

*To a man, ornithologists are tall, slender,
and bearded so that they can stand motionless
for hours, imitating kindly trees, as they
watch for birds.*

GORE VIDAL (1925–)

~~~~~~~~~~~~~~~~~~~~~~~~~

Why are chickens and pheasants terrible at flying?

If I was a bad-tempered scientist with hemorrhoids running to catch a train I'd bark: "It has to do with dietary behavior, natural selection and low-aspect-ratio wings in relation to body mass, you bloody imbecile!" and barge past you. But as I'm not, toss another log on the fire and let me explain in greater detail. Pheasants and chickens belong to an order of bird known as Galliformes, characterized by plump bodies, short wide wings and reasonably long legs. When you chase one, it will run away and will only take to the air if, say, it was being chased by Bernard Matthews and it was a choice between escaping into the nearest tree or ending up as some kind of "medallion" drowning in a pool of spaghetti hoops on the plate of an unhappy five-year-old.

Many domesticated Galliformes, including gamebirds reared for shooting, have been stuffed with so much feed they either can't fly at all or can get only a few feet off the ground. Their cousins in the wild actually aren't a great deal more adept, because they have evolved to scavenge for their food in undergrowth and on forest floors. In their original habitats, all they needed to escape the attentions of a land predator was the ability to fly as far as the nearest branch. Efficient flying was not a skill they needed to survive, hence the ungainly, explosive flapping to lift their bulky frames off the ground. Like a rower being forced to propel himself with short, stubby oars, the game bird can flap as much as it likes but it's not going to get very far.

Contrast the wings of a pheasant with those of a seabird or a long-distance wader and you will understand the difference in flying ability. Seabirds like the albatross, and other good long-distance fliers, have long, narrow, pointed wings that allow them to ride strong winds and glide at high speed with barely any effort. The vulture's wings are also long but they are wider than those of the albatross because vultures soar at lower speeds to spot sources of food. Indeed, the shape of a bird's wings tells you exactly what kind of bird it is and the life it leads: the hummingbird's are designed for hovering, those of the swallow, swift and martin for acrobatics, while your average garden bird has short, elliptical-shaped wings for quick take-off and maneuvering within the tight confines of woods and shrubbery. For game birds that spend most of the time on the ground flying is just a last resort.

Penguins prefer to swim

The penguin surrendered its power of flight over time, swapping it for an ability to dive and swim as it slowly transformed itself into an aquatic bird that lives off marine food, rather than insects, plants or meat. Today, some species spend as much as 80 percent of their lives in the wet stuff. The penguin's wings have become flippers and the light, hollow bones characteristic of a flighted bird have been replaced by heavy, dense ones to reduce buoyancy (as has happened in other birds who dive underwater to find food). The penguin has become so good at swimming that it can outpace and outmaneuver many fish. The most impressive swimmer of them all, the Michael Phelps of the avian world, is the emperor penguin, that can stay underwater for a quarter of an hour, plunge to depths of 1,640 feet and travel up to 600 miles in a single trip in search of food.

In-flight water purifying system

Albatrosses, storm petrels and shearwaters belong to a group of seabirds known as tubenoses, so called after the shape of their specially adapted nasal glands and nostril tubes, which allow them to expel the salt from the seawater they drink. The ability to drink at sea means the birds can live above the oceans for months, even years at a time, without having to touch land. Given a choice, however, they will choose fresh water over seawater.

How does a bird actually fly?

There are two forces of nature that a bird – and an airplane – must get the better of in order to fly: gravity and drag. While gravity pulls an object to the ground, drag resists its forward movement through the air. To overcome this twin resistance a bird must generate one force known as lift, that propels it clear of the ground, and another force known as thrust, to drive it through the air. Small birds are light enough to flap their wings and take off from a standing start but heavier birds such as ground-dwelling ducks, with their more solid bones and thicker plumage, need to run, or flap over the surface of the water, to generate enough forward momentum to carry them upwards, just as an airplane has to hurtle down a runway. Swans and bustards, the largest flying birds, need an even longer run-up and have to put in an even greater effort.

How a bird stays airborne is slightly more complicated and the following includes no more than an elementary outline of the biology and physics involved. The thrust to drive it through the air is generated by powerful flight muscles attached to its keel, an extension of the sternum, which acts as an anchor. The shape of the wing holds the key to maintaining the balance between lift and drag as the bird flaps, soars and glides.

The cross-section of a bird's wing is almost identical to that of an airplane and both operate according to similar aerodynamic principles. Slice a wing in half and, sideways, it looks like a teardrop. Air moving across the airfoil shape provides the necessary lift, as the pressure above the wing drops and increases below it. So long as the lift is greater than the weight of the bird and the drag caused by air resistance, the bird will stay in the air. Some birds also have a feature on each wing called an alula, which acts in the same way as the flaps on a plane wing, helping the bird to counteract the increasing drag and thus stay airborne when moving at slower speeds, for instance, when it comes in to land.

Why do geese fly in a V formation and not a B or K formation?

Not, as the village idiots in my local pub suggested, because the one at the front is the only one that knows where it's going or because birds aren't very good at reading. Many species, notably geese, ducks and pelicans, fly in V formation because it improves aerodynamics and helps save energy on long journeys, allowing them to travel many hun-

dreds or even thousands of miles further than if they flew alone, or in a different formation. The birds take advantage of the air turbulence by positioning themselves near the tips of their neighbor's wings, all flapping their wings in time with the leader and riding on the upwash generated by the downward stroke of the wing. It's a similar principle to that of the moving boat, which leaves smoother water behind its V-shaped wake. The leading bird at the point of the V has to make the greatest effort because it encounters the most air resistance, which explains why the birds take it in turns to hold that position.

Why do birds of a feather flock together?

Roughly half of the world's 10,000 bird species congregate in flocks at some time or other in spite of the risk of catastrophic annihilation caused by disease, a freak weather event or a mob of human beings armed with guns and nets. They do so for many of the same reasons that seabirds live in colonies – because the benefits for an individual bird of being in a community outweigh those of living

IN THE GARDEN

Working the bins

Even for the casual bird lover who has no intention of straying further than the end of the garden, buying a pair of half-decent binoculars will prove a worthwhile investment. Being flighty, jumpy creatures, birds tend to take to the air or retreat into the shrubbery at the first rustle of the undergrowth or crunch of a boot. Cocksure robins, sparrows and blackbirds, as well as wood pigeons, collared doves and piratical magpies, will be slower to retreat, but with most other species it's difficult to get up close to observe their fascinating behavior and mannerisms. A pair of binoculars will open up a whole new appreciation of how birds go about their daily struggle to survive. It's one thing to watch a bird pecking away at a peanut feeder, quite another to watch one busily flying back and forth to build a nest or singing from the treetops to attract a mate.

It's important to get the magnification right and not be tempted to go for the ones with the biggest numbers. The specification is given as two numbers with a cross between them (e.g., 8x30 or 7x20). The first number refers to the power of magnification, so an 8x pair will make objects look eight times closer. Birdwatchers, alone. The odds of being snatched by a predator become longer with every addition to the flock, while finding food is easier if there are more individuals on the lookout for it.

It's not always birds of the same feather that flock together because the urgency to eat transcends the species. Sparrows and starlings hunt for food in a flock all year round, but when food becomes scarce in the winter months, less gregarious birds, such as finches and tits,

however experienced, don't want the magnification to be any greater than x7 or x8 as it's difficult to keep the image stable. Forget zoom binoculars too as they don't admit enough light. The second number in the specification is the width in millimeters of the largest lens, known as the objective lens, and the larger it is the more light it lets in, making it more effective in dull weather, and at sunrise and dusk. The drawback is that the bigger the lens the heavier it is to hold, which is a consideration to bear in mind as it can be tiring to hold the arms in the binoculars position for long periods of time.

You are also better off buying a pair with a focusing wheel that doesn't need much turning to secure a quick, clear image either long-range or close up. You'll need to be fast on the draw sometimes as many birds tend not to hang around. Don't buy binoculars you haven't tried because different pairs suit different eye sockets. You don't want strange black blobs obscuring the peripheral vision. Those who wear spectacles should choose binoculars with fold-down rubber eye-cups. Most birdwatchers today prefer to use rubber-coated binoculars because they are easier to grip and are not as cold in winter.

will also team up to seek out sources, leading to the magical spectacle and sound of dozens of birds of different species swooping and chirping through woodland united by their common quest to eat.

One other reason that some birds form a flock is to keep warm. Birds need to maintain a very high body temperature of between 100 and 109 degrees Fahrenheit. This is easier to do if they huddle together in a roost at night, or in the winter. Even wrens, antisocial, solitary little buggers ordinarily, will shack up in the cold winter months, with as many as three or four dozen clustered in a nest box to share body heat.

High fliers

The highest-flying bird ever recorded was a Ruppell's griffon vulture, which collided with a commercial airliner, damaging one of the engines, over the Ivory Coast at 37,000 feet in 1973. In 1967, a wedge of whooper swans was seen at 27,000 feet by an airline pilot off the Scottish coast near the Hebrides. But bar-headed geese are probably the most frequent high fliers in the bird world. After breeding in Tibet they set off to spend the winter in the warmer climes of India, flying at over 18,000 feet to get through the Himalayas. A flock of these birds was once observed flying over the summit of Everest at least 30,000 feet above sea level.

MAKE YOUR OWN WINTER FEEDER IN MINUTES

Birds need food with a high energy content to keep them warm in the winter since their body reserves are quickly used up, particularly on very cold nights. You can help by making your own suet ball or bird cake, which is surprisingly quick and easy. Pour melted suet or lard on to a mixture of seeds, nuts, dried fruit, raw oatmeal, cheese and cake (two parts of these other foods to one part suet or lard). Stir well in a bowl and allow the goo to set in a container. An empty coconut shell or hard plastic cup makes a good feeder – or just turn the cake out on to the bird table.

Pole to Pole Without a Map

THE MYSTERY OF MIGRATION

The swallow is come!
The swallow is come!
O, fair are the seasons, and light
Are the days that she brings,
With her dusky wings,
And her bosom snowy white!

HENRY WADSWORTH LONGFELLOW

If birds have such small brains, how on earth do they know where to go when migrating thousands of miles?

How birds migrate is one of the great mysteries of nature. Some birds learn through following and observing their families, but others have no such guidance. The European cuckoo, for instance, is abandoned by its mother while still in the egg and left to be reared by a foster mother and yet, come the autumn, it takes wing for the African savannah as if it had been heading there all its life, which suggests that its navigational information has been passed on genetically. The question has been baffling and amazing people for centuries, and there is no simple answer to it. In short, birds are known or are thought to use a whole range of navigational tools and techniques that vary from species to species.

- The **sun** is one of the most important navigational aids for many species. Birds have a form of internal clock by which they can calculate the exact time the sun takes to move through the sky, whatever the latitude and whatever the time of year. Even during cloudy and poor weather, birds can still work out the sun's position by the ultraviolet rays of polarized light that humans can't see. This back-up system is not perfect, though, and many birds get lost during prolonged cloudy weather.

- They will follow visual or **geographical landmarks** such as mountain ranges, coastlines and rivers.

- Like sailors of old, they use the **stars**; on cloudy nights, some birds lose their way.

- We know from scientific experiments that some birds use the **earth's magnetic field** to steer them to their destination. The birds fitted with little magnets to disrupt perception of the earth's magnetic field all got lost. Scientists found tiny particles of a magnetic mineral called magnetite in the head of some birds, leading them to believe they had an internal compass of some sort: the mineral can detect the earth's magnetic field, which gives the birds the ability to locate the position of magnetic north.

- Birds also orient themselves by detecting **infrasound**, a noise with a frequency so low humans can't hear it. The crash of wind and sea against land generates infrasound, which travels very long distances and helps migrant birds identify the landscape ahead.

- Some birds are born with a navigating **instinct** that has programmed them to head in a particular direction at certain times of year.

❝ Man feels himself an infinity above those creatures who stand, zoologically, only one step below him, but every human being looks up to the birds. They suit the fancy of us all. What they feel they can voice, as we try to; they court and nest, they battle with the elements, they are torn by two opposing impulses, a love of home and a passion for far places. Only with birds do we share so much emotion . . . birds seem to us like emissaries of another world which exists about us and above us, but into which, earthbound, we cannot penetrate. ❞

WRITER DONALD CULROSS PEATTIE (1935)

Arctic tern: the long-distance champion

No other creature on earth sees as much sun as the tiny Arctic tern. In August, this remarkable seabird, not much bigger than a blackbird, leaves its breeding territories in the Arctic at the top of the planet and sets out on an epic journey to its winter quarters in the Antarctic at the bottom. It will follow one of three main routes: down western Europe and the West African coast; across the Atlantic and down the eastern seaboard of South America; or from northwest Canada down the west coast of the Americas. All three groups then cross the wild and stormy Great Southern Ocean. By the time it has returned to the Arctic, the tern will have flown an astonishing 25,000 miles. One of the reasons why it is able to achieve this feat is that, like many seabirds, it has adapted to feed and drink at sea, allowing it to refuel on the go.

(A growing shortage of fish stocks is starting to threaten some colonies.) One Arctic tern, ringed as a chick on the Farne Islands off the Northumberland coast in England, reached Melbourne in Australia just three months after it fledged.

Only the sooty shearwaters can rival the Arctic terns for long-distance migration. Every year, they set off on a remarkable circular journey that takes them from their breeding grounds in the Southern Ocean – including a large colony in the Falkland Islands – up the western side of the Pacific and Atlantic Oceans, to the coastlines near the Arctic Circle where they spend June and July. From there they head east, then south down the eastern side of the oceans to reach their nesting areas in November. Manx shearwaters, which breed in great numbers around the western coasts of the British Isles, are thought to make the same journey, but anticlockwise, heading down the Atlantic coast of South America to their winter quarters and then crossing the Atlantic to return via the African coast.

At the other end of the scale there are some species such as the wallcreeper and mountain quail that migrate no further than up and down the mountain or hill where they live.

Autumn Birds

The wild duck startles like a sudden thought,
And heron slow as if it might be caught.
The flopping crows on weary wings go by
And grey beard jackdaws noising as they fly.
The crowds of starnels whizz and hurry by,
And darken like a clod the evening sky.
The larks like thunder rise and suthy round,
Then drop and nestle in the stubble ground.
The wild swan hurries hight and noises loud
With white neck peering to the evening clowd.
The weary rooks to distant woods are gone.
With lengths of tail the magpie winnows on
To neighbouring tree, and leaves the distant crow
While small birds nestle in the edge below.

JOHN CLARE

Why do so many birds go to the incredible effort and risk of crossing half the planet twice a year?

It seems obvious that birds might want to leave North America and northern Europe in the cold months of winter and go in search of food, but it's odd that they bother making the long and hazardous journey back every year from the warmth of Central and Southern America and Africa, where food can be found all year round. Leaving aside the question of why they do it, even the basic facts of migration are a fairly recent discovery. The general understanding used to be that many birds hibernated. Highly intelligent, sensible people, including the eighteenth-century English writer Dr. Samuel Johnson, even believed that swallows spent the winter at the bottom of rivers. Birds such as warblers, flycatchers, swallows and many hummingbirds are common sights in North America in the warmer months, but it's fairer to say that they are visitors from Central and South America rather than residents here. They came north in the first place owing to the pressure of competition for food and mates. During the last Ice Age, much of northern hemisphere was covered in glaciers and ice sheets, and most birds and mammals lived in the south. When the ice retreated toward the Arctic, it left behind a lovely damp landscape rich in plants and buzzing with insects in the warmer months. Gradually, the birds and other animals headed north; some of them became permanent residents, but those birds that didn't like the cold started coming for the summer and returned south for the winter. Over millions of years these species redesigned themselves for the long journeys, growing longer wings, learning navigational skills and developing the ability to store fat to give them the necessary energy. Summer in the more northerly latitudes provides not only an abundance of insects but also much longer days, which means birds have more time to forage and feed their chicks in the breeding season. There are also fewer predators. Although migration is a dangerous enterprise and many birds will die on the way, on balance, it makes evolutionary sense for them to shuttle thousands of miles back and forth each year.

~~~~~~~~~

Swallows certainly sleep all winter. A number of them conglobulate together, by flying round and round, and then all in a heap throw themselves under water, and lye in the bed of a river.
ENGLISH WRITER SAMUEL JOHNSON (1709–84)

~~~~~~~~~

700,000 miles to the gallon

The tiny blackpoll warbler, no larger than a blue tit, doubles its weight from about 11g to 21g to sustain it on its astonishing annual journey from Canada and the northeastern United States to South America. The non-stop flight, which is made by five billion warblers every autumn, covers between three and six thousand miles down the eastern seaboard of North America. By the time the bird arrives, about 90 hours after taking to the air, it will have flapped its wings roughly four million times, having expended no more energy than the amount to be had from a small Mars bar. It has been calculated that if the warbler burned up oil rather than fat, it would be doing over 700,000 miles to the gallon.

That's just silly

For centuries it was believed that the barnacle goose hatched out of the barnacles growing on rocks along the British coast. Nor was this a conviction held only by the more dim-witted Britons in the Middle Ages – it wasn't until 1891, when the first nest was found in Greenland, that the myth was finally exploded. The study of migration had barely begun even then, and the old belief, which now seems so ludicrous, arose out of the fact these geese were never seen in the summer.

That both the barnacles and the geese were black and white and a bit mottled, and they appeared in different seasons, apparently clinched it for our ancestors. If any Catholics knew the truth, they weren't going to let on. Barnacles being seafood, the goose that issued from a barnacle was counted as a fish and could therefore be eaten on Fridays and during Lent, when meat was forbidden by the Church.

"" Yet this little winged seraph [barn swallow], if I may so speak, who, in a few days, and at will, can pass from the borders of the arctic regions to the torrid zone, is forced, when winter approaches, to descend to the bottoms of lakes, rivers, and mill-ponds, to bury itself in the mud with eels and snapping turtles; or to creep ingloriously into a cavern, a rat-hole, or a hollow tree, there to doze, with snakes, toads, and other reptiles, until the return of spring! Is not this true, ye wise men of Europe and America, who have published so many credible narratives on this subject? The geese, the ducks, the cat-bird, and even the wren, which creeps about our outhouses in summer like a mouse, are all acknowledged to be migratory, and to pass to southern regions at the approach of winter: the swallow alone, on whom Heaven has conferred superior powers of wing, must sink in torpidity at the bottom of our rivers, or doze all winter in the caverns of the earth . . . should I affirm, that thousands of people in the neighborhood of this city, regularly undergo the same semi-annual submersion, – that I myself had fished up a whole family of these from the bottom of Schuylkill, where they had lain torpid all winter, carried them home, and brought them all comfortably to themselves again – should I even publish this in the learned pages of the Transactions of our Philosophical Society, who would believe me? Is, then, the organization of a swallow less delicate than that of a man? Can a bird, whose vital functions are destroyed by a short privation of pure air and its usual food, sustain, for six months, a situation where the most robust man would perish in a few hours, or minutes? Away with such absurdities! they are unworthy of a serious refutation. I should be pleased to meet with a man who has been personally more conversant with birds than myself, who has followed them in their wide and devious routes – studied their various manners – mingled with and marked their peculiarities more than I have done; yet the miracle of a resuscitated swallow, in the depth of winter, from the bottom of a mill-pond, is, I confess, a phenomenon in ornithology that I have never met with. 🙶

ALEXANDER WILSON, AMERICAN ORNITHOLOGY (1808–14)

How do birds know when it's time to leave?

Hormonal changes and an intuitive or genetically inherited feel for the seasons tell birds when to up-nest and leave. Shorter days, a drop in air temperature and a decrease in local food supply are all signs telling the birds it's time to move on. But for many songbirds the trigger is a huge increase in appetite to fatten up for the long journey ahead. Timing its run is crucial to a bird's survival: go too early and there may not be

~~~~~~~~~~

*Migration study, complex
though it is, still depends –
and always will depend –
on the observatory and field
man, the island lover, the
cape haunter and the
sandwich eater.*

JAMES FISHER, *SEA BIRDS*

~~~~~~~~~~

enough food ready at the other end, but go too late and bad weather may claim it en route.

Birds are excellent weather forecasters and they wait for a period of high pressure with clear skies and favorable or light winds before setting out. Some of them can sense even the smallest change in barometric pressure and they will react to changes in the weather well before there is any visible sign of them.

Where do all the birds go?

Roughly three quarters of all the 700 or so bird species that exist in North America are migratory to some extent. For some, such as the grouse and quail, this will mean nothing more exhausting than moving up and down a mountainside, but for most birds the migration journey is an adventure that will take them hundreds and thousands of miles. Up to 250 species are considered neo-tropical, meaning that they winter in Mexico, Central and South America and the Caribbean, and they include most swallows, wood warblers, vireos and flycatchers as well as many birds of prey and shorebirds.

Twice a year, five billion birds pass through the major North American migration routes to and from their nesting sites: the four "flyways" are known as the Atlantic, the Mississippi, the Central and the Pacific.

Bird similes
Eat like a bird
Bald as a coot
Eyes like a hawk
Like a duck to water
Free as a bird
Like a headless chicken
Proud as a peacock
As wise as an owl
As graceful as a swan
As happy as a lark
Sing like a bird
Crazy as a loon
Like water off a duck's back
As the crow flies

A Manx shearwater, transported from its home in Wales and released in America, was back in its burrow on Skokholm Island off the Pembrokeshire coast 24 hours before the letter arrived announcing it had set off.

Over Panama, where the continental landmass shrinks to its narrowest point, the birds from the four routes merge into one and then spread out again across South America. Overland migration tends to be along routes with no major mountains or water areas to cross and offer the longest and widest field of sight. Birds have learned to wend their way through myriad passes and valleys to continue their vital journeys. Large, broad-winged birds, such as eagles, vultures, kites, buzzards and storks, rely on thermal columns of hot air in the atmosphere when they travel long distances. Thermals only occur over land, where heat from the sun-warmed earth rises high into the sky, to the delight of birds and hang gliders alike. Soaring is a great way of saving energy as the bird barely needs to flap its wings. The wind all but carries it to its destination. Without the wind, these migratory species would find it impossible to cross large bodies of water as they cannot sustain active flight over more than short periods. Another consideration is that, whereas most migrating songbirds fatten up before setting out on their journey, birds of prey need to hunt along the way to maintain their energy levels. Of the billions of birds migrating between Europe and Africa, the Mediterranean presents a major obstacle to soaring birds and so they have learned to cross it at its narrowest points. At peak migration times, massive numbers of birds of prey and storks pass through Gibraltar and Istanbul where the sea is at its narrowest.

The annual odyssey of the bar-tailed godwit

The bar-tailed godwit, a large shorebird, makes the longest nonstop migration of any bird when it sets off from its breeding grounds in Alaska and heads south to winter in New Zealand and eastern Australia – a distance of 7,000 miles for those flying farthest. Most long-distance migratory birds stop to feed along the way to replenish their flagging energy reserves, but before setting out the godwit puts on vast amounts of fat and muscle, then shrinks its digestive systems for the flight. Scientists are not sure why the 130,000 birds are prepared to make the annual odyssey when there is an alternative route via Asia offering refueling stops. The theories are that in doing it the hard way they are avoiding predators and diseases or getting to their winter homes quicker.

How do hundreds of millions of birds survive crossing the Sahara?

The Sahara desert is a vast stretch of baking sand and rock, the size of the United States and expanding by the year. Stretching from one side of northern Africa to the other, it is 1,000 miles wide north to south at its narrowest point, water sources are limited to a handful of oases, the daytime temperatures are blisteringly hot and at night it is perishingly cold. The Sahara is one of the most inhospitable regions of the planet but twice a year huge populations of little swallows, swifts, cuckoos, flycatchers and warblers somehow manage to cross it. How they achieve this remarkable feat of endurance is not yet understood. The birds emerge into the more temperate climes on either side of the desert exhausted, starving and dehydrated, but after a few days of voracious eating and drinking they are up and on their way

Random fate
Of six Brent geese fitted with radio-tracking tags in Northern Ireland in May 2002, only one was known to have survived to the following winter, two fell victim to Arctic foxes and one, called Kerry, was found three months later in the freezer of an Inuit hunter on the remote Cornwallis Island off Canada.

once more. The journey stretches the birds to the limit and if it was much longer they would start to die en route – an alarming development that some scientists believe is already happening. The numbers of birds from sub-Saharan Africa that arrive in Britain for the summer have crashed in recent years and ornithologists believe that desertification of more swaths of previously fertile African land is one of the likely reasons behind the fall, along with the introduction of pesticides and new farming practices across the continent.

> Because the road is rough and long
> Shall we despise the skylark's song?
> **ENGLISH WRITER ANNE BRONTË (1820–49)**

Twice a year, migratory birds kept in captivity display a restlessness known by its German term *zugunruhe*, proving that in many species the migratory urge and the knowledge of when and in which direction to go are genetically inherited. At exactly the same time of year that their cousins in the wild are migrating to their other home, caged birds flap their wings and anxiously hop about on their perches. Many even point themselves in the direction in which they would be heading.

Fatal attraction

Tall buildings and fog can be a fatal combination for the billions of migrating songbirds that travel by night each year to and from their nesting areas in North America.

The US Fish and Wildlife Service estimates that as many as 50 million birds are killed every year by "tower kill" after being drawn to the lights on communication towers when the visibility is poor. Birds use the stars to help navigate their route but if they cannot see them through the fog they will head toward other elevated light sources. More than 225 species, some of them listed as endangered, have been affected by this very modern phenomenon. The worst recorded incident so far took place in Kansas in 1998 when between 5,000 and 10,000 Lapland longspurs – sparrow-like birds that fly in massive flocks – crashed into the guy wires around a 400-foot radio transmitter. The disoriented birds, who breed in the high Arctic and winter across much of the United States, circled the structure for hours before colliding with it and crashing into a heap of carcasses below.

WHEN TO SPOT MASS MIGRATIONS

Most migrating waders and songbirds travel at night and land to rest within an hour of sunrise. If you want to see these spectacular migrations, set your alarm for just before dawn. The birds travel under darkness because there is less chance of an attack by predators, they can forage for food during the day and the much cooler night-time temperatures reduce the risk of overheating or dehydration. Flying is easier too because typically the air is more stable than during the day when hotter air rises from the earth and the wind direction is more erratic. The night-fliers normally set out just before dusk in order to get their bearings from the setting sun and then plot their route according to the position of the moon and stars. Scientists have carried out experiments inside planetariums in which the birds behaved as if on a real migration.

No Nightingale did ever chaunt
More welcome notes to weary bands
Of travellers in some shady haunt,
Among Arabian sands:
A voice so thrilling ne'er was heard
In spring-time from the Cuckoo-bird,
Breaking the silence of the seas
Among the farthest Hebrides
WILLIAM WORDSWORTH

O Cuckoo! shall I call thee bird,
Or but a wandering voice?
WILLIAM WORDSWORTH

A swift decline

Its cylindrical body has earned it the nickname the "flying cigar," but ironically the chimney swift could be extinguished in North America as it struggles once again to replace its constantly disappearing habitat.

These aerodynamic maestros began nesting in chimneys when their former homes in the hollows of trees disappeared under the settlers' ax. Swifts need deep shafts in which to nest because they cannot perch like songbirds, but recent changes in chimney design and the demolition of old buildings have depressed their numbers once again.

True hope is swift, and flies with swallow's wings;
Kings it makes gods, and meaner creatures kings.
WILLIAM SHAKESPEARE (1564–1616)

WAYS TO HELP CHIMNEY SWIFTS

- If you have a brick or clay chimney, keep the top open and the damper closed from March through October to provide a nest site. Metal chimneys should be permanently capped to prevent birds and other wildlife from being trapped.

- Have your chimney cleaned before the chimney swifts return from their winter home in South America in early March.

- Work with local conservation groups to construct chimney swift towers.

- Choose a chimney sweep that doesn't offer "bird removal."

(Advice from the North American chimney swift nest site research project.)

See! from the brake the whirring pheasant springs,
And mounts exulting on triumphant wings:
Short is his joy; he feels the fiery wound,
Flutters in blood, and panting beats the ground.
ENGLISH POET ALEXANDER POPE (1688–1744)

Slaughter in the Med

In recent years, conservation groups have been turning up the political heat on the governments of southern Europe to bring an end to the annual slaughter of millions of birds, including many increasingly rare species such as the lesser kestrel, osprey and purple heron. Hunters in Malta, Cyprus, Italy, Portugal and parts of France are seen as the worst offenders, wiping out the birds in the migration season in the name of sport. In days gone by, the hunters killed for food; today they do it for fun, taxidermy and target practice. Malta alone has nearly 12,000 hunters and over 4,500 trappers in a population of just 400,000. As a direct result of the persecution, only 21 species of bird breed in Malta today.

Many of the birds are protected by law but it is difficult to stop the hunters due to a lack of political will, opposition from the hunters and trappers and a shortage of law enforcement officers on the ground. Conservation organizations in the north of Europe argue that it is their business to get involved because many of the species being killed are their summer visitors making their way to or from their winter homes. Live-trapping is also widely practiced so the hunters can use the birds as caged pets or as decoys. Trapping methods include sticks covered in glue that fixes the bird when it lands on them, nets, snares and lures – such as live decoys, food bait or sound recordings of bird song.

Many migrant birds that are not usually gregarious will flock together before and/or during migration for the same reasons that social or colony birds do it all the time. As a team, they have more chance of seeking out food sources and finding the way to their destination, and each individual has less chance of being taken by a predator.

Bird wrecks

Although many birds are able to forecast weather in the short term, there is little they can do if they are hit by a storm midway through their migratory journey. The strong winds may blow seabirds hundreds, even thousands of miles off course in an event

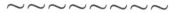

known as a "bird wreck." Many will never complete their journey, dying of exhaustion in their struggle to get back on course. Others will be blown off their usual routes over the open seas and on to land where they will settle for a few days' rest and wait for the storm to pass before trying to reorient themselves. These can be exciting moments for bird-watchers as they flock to see unfamiliar visitors to their

You must not know too much, or be too precise or scientific about birds and trees and flowers and water-craft; a certain free margin, and even vagueness – perhaps ignorance, credulity – helps your enjoyment of these things.

WALT WHITMAN

shores. Ringing evidence has shown that, from time to time, some species from the Americas, blown over to Britain in a period of extreme weather, have chosen to join their foreign cousins on the winter migration to Africa and have returned across the Atlantic the following spring. A "wreck" is distinct from a "fall" in which migrating birds, usually songbirds, are forced to descend on to the land below and wait for a break in the bad weather before continuing their journey.

Robin Redbreast

Good-bye, good-bye to Summer!
  For Summer's nearly done;
The garden smiling faintly,
  Cool breezes in the sun;
Our Thrushes now are silent,
  Our Swallows flown away, –
But Robin's here, in coat of brown,
  With ruddy breast-knot gay.
    Robin, Robin Redbreast,
      O Robin dear!
    Robin sings so sweetly
      In the falling of the year.
Bright yellow, red, and orange,
  The leaves come down in hosts;

The trees are Indian Princes,
  But soon they'll turn to Ghosts;
The scanty pears and apples
  Hang russet on the bough;
It's Autumn, Autumn, Autumn late,
  'Twill soon be Winter now.
    Robin, Robin Redbreast,
      O Robin dear!
    And welaway! my Robin,
      For pinching days are near.

The fire-side for the cricket,
  The wheatstack for the mouse,
When trembling night-winds whistle
  And moan all round the house.
The frosty ways like iron,
  The branches plumed with snow, –
Alas! in winter dead and dark,
  Where can poor Robin go?
    Robin, Robin Redbreast,
      O Robin dear!
    And a crumb of bread for Robin,
      His little heart to cheer!

IRISH POET WILLIAM ALLINGHAM (1824–89)

Just Behave

THE REMARKABLE BEHAVIOR OF BIRDS

Stocking the pantry for winter

Birds migrate in order to find a regular source of food, but those that stay behind must find other ways of surviving nature's less bountiful seasons. Unlike many mammals, birds cannot go long periods without food because they burn up so much energy keeping warm, flying and foraging. For century after century, in the days before refrigeration, canning and other advanced methods of preservation, man had to be inventive and resourceful in making the most of nature's harvest in fall for the coming winter. In exactly the same way, only for hundreds of thousands of years earlier, a number of bird species, unwilling to make the hazardous journeys to and from warmer climes, developed often remarkable storage techniques to see them through the less productive, colder months of the year. Hoarding, practiced in North America by various woodpeckers, nuthatches, some jays and Clark's nutcrackers, is a survival strategy that comes with its own risks as stores of food may rot or be plundered by others. But for the species that have adopted and refined it, it is no more perilous than either migration or the only other alternative on offer, which is scavenging on winter's leaner offerings, as natural selection has led ptarmigans and chickadees to do.

Scientists have long been fascinated by the phenomenon of hoarding because it shows that birds are capable of (a) making plans for the future and (b) remembering where they have hidden their food. Hoarding birds keep their seeds and nuts in dozens of different places, while the Clark's nutcracker stores over 30,000 pinyon seeds in as many as 700 separate sites. How the birds can recall the precise locations, often several months later, is not yet fully understood, but experiments with marsh tits have shown the birds remembered them by reference to nearby objects. Scrub and pinyon jays, and Clark's nutcrackers to a lesser extent, are thought to be able to find their buried acorns by the orientation of the sun, even on a cloudy day.

The way birds stockpile their winter supplies varies from species to species. Nutcrackers and jays tend to store acorns, nuts, seeds, cones and other items in the earth or under loose ground cover, as well as in niches and cracks above ground level. Nutcrackers will bury as many as 100,000 seeds each fall, and they have a pouch under the tongue in which they can carry up to 50 seeds back to their storage sites. Acorn woodpeckers store acorns in one or two sites, usually dead trunks and branches, close to the heart of the group territory. The cache is known as a granary and each one may contain up to 50,000. The woodpeckers will defend their supplies vigorously, but they take the added precaution of hammering the acorns so hard that most robbers struggle to extract them.

The Truth

Since I have seen a bird one day,
His head pecked more than half away;
That hopped about, with but one eye,
Ready to fight again, and die –
Ofttimes since then their private lives
Have spoilt that joy their music gives.

So when I see this robin now,
Like a red apple on the bough,
And question why he sings so strong,
For love, or for the love of song;
Or sings, maybe, for that sweet rill
Whose silver tongue is never still –

Ah, now there comes this thought unkind,
Born of the knowledge in my mind:
He sings in triumph that last night
He killed his father in a fight;
And now he'll take his mother's blood –
The last strong rival for his food.

W. H. DAVIES
(WRITING ABOUT THE EUROPEAN ROBIN)

Never trust a bird with a beard

The bearded tit is an odd little bird, and its habits, evolutionary history and flight are just as quirky as its appearance and as amusing as its name. For a start, it's not really a tit. It belongs to a family of birds called parrotbills that live in Asia. Secondly, it doesn't have a beard. The plump little reedbed-dweller with the jaunty undulating flight is not closely related to any other European species, and it has what people whose job it is to describe the appearance of birds call a "moustache," in the form of a black stripe running down each side of its face from the eye, like non-waterproof mascara.

The bearded tit even eats oddly. In the breeding season it eats insects, and can be seen shimmying up and down reed stems (if you're lucky, that is, because it's a shy creature). When the seeds start to fall to the ground, it scratches around in the dirt, just like a chicken. The switch from eating soft juicy insects to hard seeds forces the walls of its digestive system to develop incredibly strong muscle tissue. To help grind down and mince up the hard-shelled seeds, the bearded tit will swallow up to 400 tiny pieces of grit, giving it a bloated appearance in the winter. They have always been vulnerable to severe winters, but their numbers have declined sharply in recent years despite the milder climate.

Hedgerow hooligans

Until very recently the black-billed magpie was considered the same species as the Eurasian magpie, but scientists have found subtle differences. What they will always have in common, however, is an unattractive habit of stealing and eating the eggs and nestlings of other birds. Magpies used to be a favorite target for farmers, hunters and gamekeepers and many still see them as vermin. There are frequent calls for a cull of magpie numbers, but in the absence of proper research showing their impact on other species, conservation bodies are reluctant to act against this noisy crow. Black-billed magpies, a common sight across much of North America, are ingenious opportunists that will even steal food from other birds. They also eat ticks from the backs of large mammals, such as deer and moose, and will pick at the animals' open sores. In the past the distinctive black and white birds with the long tail followed Native Americans, living off the scraps from their bison hunts, but today it is the car they follow. With more and more carrion littering our roads, magpies and other scavengers are enjoying a year-round ready-made meal in areas where previously their numbers were probably kept down by a lack of food in the winter.

The Dying Swan

The plain was grassy, wild and bare,
Wide, wild, and open to the air,
Which had built up everywhere
   An under-roof of doleful gray.
With an inner voice the river ran,
Adown it floated a dying swan,
   And loudly did lament.
It was the middle of the day.
Ever the weary wind went on,
   And took the reed-tops as it went.

Some blue peaks in the distance rose,
And white against the cold-white sky,
Shone out their crowning snows.
   One willow over the river wept,
And shook the wave as the wind did sigh;
Above in the wind was the swallow,
   Chasing itself at its own wild will,
   And far thro' the marish green and still
   The tangled water-courses slept,
Shot over with purple, and green, and yellow.

The wild swan's death-hymn took the soul
Of that waste place with joy
Hidden in sorrow: at first to the ear
The warble was low, and full and clear;
And floating about the under-sky,
Prevailing in weakness, the coronach stole
Sometimes afar, and sometimes anear;
But anon her awful jubilant voice,
With a music strange and manifold,
Flow'd forth on a carol free and bold;
As when a mighty people rejoice
With shawms, and with cymbals, and harps of gold,
And the tumult of their acclaim is roll'd
Thro' the open gates of the city afar,
To the shepherd who watcheth the evening star.
And the creeping mosses and clambering weeds,
And the willow-branches hoar and dank,
And the wavy swell of the soughing reeds,
And the wave-worn horns of the echoing bank,
And the silvery marish-flowers that throng
The desolate creeks and pools among,
Were flooded over with eddying song.

ENGLISH POET ALFRED, LORD TENNYSON (1809–92)

A squadron of Shitfires

The fieldfare, a thrush that flies
from Scandinavia to spend the winter
in Britain, has a unique way of
repelling predators: it shits on them.
From a great height, needless to say.
If a crow, magpie, jay or bird of prey
tries to raid their loosely spread
colonies in the woods during the
breeding season, the fieldfares
scramble to the skies like a squadron
of Spitfires, their siren squawks filling
the air, and proceed to launch a series

of dive-bombing sorties, each time unloading a squirt of shit on the intruders. Sometimes they will even ram into them. The attack is more than just an unpleasant inconvenience for the predator – it can be fatal, albeit in rare cases. The uric acid in the shit has a corrosive effect on plumage, and without its feathers a bird is as good as dead. British predators need have no fears, however, because the attacks normally only take place during the breeding season in Scandinavia, although occasionally fieldfares will deploy the same "bombing" tactics to defend a favorite feeding ground.

The fieldfare is also one of the earliest risers in the avian community, appearing up to 90 minutes before dawn, according to the people whose job it is to get up in the middle of the night to check these things.

The highwayman of the high seas

The skua, and its near-identical twin the jager, are the scourge of sea-cliff colonies, built to mug, rob and kill. With their powerful bills and clawed webs, these avian pirates worked out fairly early in their evolution that life would be far easier if they let other seabirds do the often exhausting job of finding the fish. They will hunt their own food too, but often decide to save energy by waiting back near land for a tern, puffin or other unsuspecting parent to return with a mouthful of goodies for its young. They then intercept and rob the hardworking hunter at bill point. Other victims may be forced to regurgitate their food and may occasionally become prey themselves for some species of these avian pirates. You too might be reluctant, at the end of a 200-mile roundtrip to feed your young, to hand over your provisions to a violent intruder waiting on your doorstep, but most birds are no match for a skua if it comes down to a straight one-on-one scrap. One notable exception is the gannet, the largest seabird in the North Atlantic, that will give every bit as good as it gets, aided by its long sharp beak, which has been adapted for skewering fish when it plunges into the sea from 100 feet.

Dance for your dinner

The ring-billed gull and the herring gull have become familiar sights on garbage dumps and sports fields. Screeching scavengers that eat virtually anything and rob other birds of their food may not be the most popular birds in town, but if you're looking for positives they do perform a charming dance routine. When it's particularly wet underfoot, look out for gulls, running on the spot on sports fields and other stretches of open grass. The stomping is thought to mimic the drumming of rain and forces the worms to come to the surface to avoid drowning in the soupy morass created by the boogying bird.

> A mute swan is so called because unlike other swans, it makes little noise and doesn't call in flight.

Why do some birds like to bathe in the dust at the side of roads?

"Dusting" is common among birds living in arid climates, but some birds in temperate climates, such as larks, sparrows and wrens, will also wash in dust if there's no water to be found. Dusting is part of a bird's rigorous preening regime. Most birds store oil in a gland under their tail, and they rub it over their plumage with their beaks.

Bird sayings
A bird in the hand is worth two in the bush.
Birds of a feather flock together.
The early bird catches the worm.
To kill two birds with one stone.
You're counting your chickens before they've hatched.
The chickens have come home to roost.

When they want to clean the feathers on their head, they wipe the oil on their feet and then smear it on their heads. The oil has antibacterial, fungicidal and waterproofing qualities. Scientists believe that dusting helps birds rid the feathers of parasites, debris and excess oil.

Why do birds sunbathe?

Some birds, notably blackbirds but also others including pigeons, thrushes, robins and sparrows, can occasionally be seen sunbathing, lying face down on a warm, safe spot such as a roof, with wings and tail feathers outstretched. Quite why they do this is not fully understood but the experts suspect it is related to the maintenance of their plumage. There are four theories: (1) the sun's rays help the spread of preening oil through the feathers; (2) parasites are lured to the surface where the bird can pick them off more easily; (3) the ultraviolet light converts chemicals in the preening oil into vitamin D; (4) it may simply be that the birds are using the sun to help them save energy, by boosting the high body temperature they need to maintain.

There was an Old Man with a beard,
Who said, "It is just as I feared! –
   Two Owls and a Hen,
   Four Larks and a Wren,
Have all built their nests in my beard!"
ENGLISH WRITER EDWARD LEAR (1812–88)

Why do some birds rub themselves with ants?

Over 200 species of birds indulge in the weird activity of "anting," spreading themselves over an anthill or nest and letting the insects run amok in their feathers. Some birds pick up the ants in their beaks and rub them over their feathers. Either way, the birds often seem to reach a point of ecstasy while they are anting. Starlings and blue jays are two common species that have been observed anting. Experts believe the formic acid released by the ants may help kill off lice and other parasites, but as with so much bird behavior, it's still a mystery.

Birds who do what their names suggest

Turnstone
Woodpecker
Treecreeper
Dipper
Nuthatch
Flycatcher
Wagtail
Shoveler

Be very wary of the cassowary

The third largest flightless bird after the ostrich and the emu, the cassowary is a shy creature living deep in the forests of northern Australia and Papua New Guinea, but if provoked or cornered it will lash out with its powerful legs and claws. Regarded as the most fearsome bird on the planet, it has been known to disembowel a man with a single kick.

Why do some birds like to spread their wings over a smoking chimney pot?

Birds such as rooks and starlings can sometimes be seen perching over smoking chimneys with their wings fully extended, and some have even been seen to rub themselves with a smoking cigarette butt. On rare occasions both houses and treetops have been set on fire when a bird has taken a burning butt back to its nest. Just as they are still baffled by the mysteries of anting and sunbathing, scientists have yet to crack the puzzle of why some birds like to "smoke-bathe," but as with the other two bizarre activities, it is probably to do with grooming and ridding themselves of irritating parasites.

Why do seabirds, often millions of them, form giant cities on cliffs and rocks?

In spite of drawing the attention of predators by the incredible noise and commotion, not to mention the hideous stink of their guano, seabirds are safer living in great numbers and have a better chance of breeding successfully than if they split up into pairs. Even the most ferocious predator will turn tail under attack from a thousand screeching gulls or gannets. The birds are also playing a percentage game, knowing that the greater their number, the smaller the chance they have of falling victim to a raid. The same principle applies to crime on a crowded subway train – there are only so many pockets a pickpocket can rifle, so the busier the train the less likely it is that any individual passenger will be robbed. What's more, as any twenty-something at a nightclub will testify, a crowded dance floor is a better place to find a date than a phone booth. The noise and excitement of a sea colony stimulates the ovaries and testes of the birds. The third advantage of living in a giant community is that the birds are able to pool their resources to help locate passing shoals of fish. It should be noted that not all birds enjoy living in these cliff-face cities as it means sharing their living quarters with some extremely ill-mannered neighbors such as fulmars, skuas and great black-backed gulls. The truth is that these birds have little choice because often there just aren't enough cliffs to go around.

Why do parrots lick clay?

Wild parrots, parakeets and macaws eat a lot of nuts and seeds that contain poisonous chemicals and it is thought that they lick and gnaw clay to help absorb the toxins. Along the banks of the Amazonian river network are many stretches of clay deposits known as "licks" where the colorful birds congregate in their hundreds. Clay is rich in alkaline minerals, including calcium compounds, which help counteract stomach acid and aid digestion.

Why do owls and other birds of prey get "mobbed" by dozens of other birds?

In a nutshell, "small bird syndrome," a phenomenon of animal behavior similar to "short man syndrome," aka the Napoleon Complex, in which the male of the species *Homo sapiens* lashes out at his bigger rivals in order to prove that his physical shortcomings are no bar to virility. In the avian world, the smaller creatures have more pressing and forgivable reasons for taking on the local bully. They do this as a group, swirling around the predator in a mad, squawking, screeching frenzy and driving it out of the immediate vicinity. Differences between species are set aside as all manner of small birds including blackbirds, robins, finches and tits join forces to see off an intruder. Most mobbing takes place in the breeding season, especially once the chicks have hatched and are starting to fledge. Owls and other birds of prey, magpies, crows and jays often find themselves on the receiving end of a mobbing, but other animals including cats, foxes and even humans also get attacked. Gulls, terns and crows are among the most ferocious and alarming of mobbers.

Nice family

The fulmar's name means "foul gull" and comes from its habit of spewing dark smelly gunk over unwelcome visitors. Just as a fieldfare will shit on a predator to drive it away, the fulmar will spit out oily gunge from its stomach with the accuracy of a champion darts player. The disgusting substance has the same corrosive effect on a bird's plumage as a fieldfare's flying turd. The chicks of the fulmar, a relation of the altogether better-mannered albatross, can do their own gobbing after just 14 days.

> The plural of goose is geese,
> But the plural of moose ain't meese,
> And the plural of noose ain't neese,
> But the plural of goose – is geese.
>
> **ROLAND YOUNG (1887–1953)**

Screech for the sky

In 1621, a famous aerial battle took place between two huge flocks of starlings over the city of Cork in southern Ireland. It lasted for three days and led to the deaths of thousands of birds, whose mutilated bodies fell into the streets and fields to the astonishment of the people watching below. A man called Nicholas Bourne collected testimonies from witnesses to the battle, which darkened the sky and filled the air with demonic screeching between October 12 and 14. He published a pamphlet titled *The Wonderfull Battell of Starelings*.

One flock of starlings had gathered in the east and one in the west of the city, bringing the two into conflict over the territory they each wanted to claim for food and roosting. The battle began with a series of skirmishes and what appeared to onlookers to be a series of reconnaissance missions by small squadrons of birds from each camp. After a few days, the main fighting erupted when both flocks took to the skies and flew straight at each other. Bourne describes what happened: "Upon a strange sound and noise made as

THE
WONDERFVLL
Battell of STARELINGS:
Fought at the Citie of *Corke* in *Ireland*, the 11. and 14. of October laſt paſt. 1621.

As it hath been incredibly enformed by diuers Noble-men, and others of the ſaid Kingdome, &c.

LONDON,
Printed for N.B. 1622.

well on the one side as on the other, they forthwith at one instant took wing, and so mounting up into the skies, encountered one another with such a terrible shock, as the sound amazed the whole citie . . . Upon this sudden and fierce encounter, there fell down into the citie, and into the rivers, multitudes of starelings, some with wings broken, some with legs and necks broken, some with eyes picked out, some their bills thrust into the breasts and sides of their adversaries."

The battle raged until dusk and the following day it erupted again, this time 400 miles away over the Thames estuary in London. Passengers on the Woolwich ferryboat reported seeing "infinite multitudes of starlings fighting in all violent manner together, with a crow or raven flying betwixt them." The following morning the birds were back over Cork where "More dead birds rained down upon the streets and houses, but this time among them were found the mangled bodies of a kite, a raven, and a crow." The fighting continued into the afternoon until, in an instant, both flocks, now considerably smaller and worn out by their exertions, disappeared in different directions.

Eight months later the city was ravaged by fire after a series of lightning strikes in a storm. The feeling among the locals was that the two incidents were linked and that they were being punished for their wickedness. A long ballad called "The Lamentable Burning of the City of Corke" by an unknown author was published not long afterward.

Do birds that attack windows have mental health problems?

If you have ever seen a drunk fighting his own reflection in a shop window, then you will have some idea of what our garden birds are doing when they swoop up to the kitchen window and start pecking at it furiously. It can be quite an alarming spectacle, with the bird seemingly trying to get into the house – as if an extra from Hitchcock's *The Birds* has escaped from the film set and come to peck out our eyes. But in fact it is simply a case of mistaken identity. Very mistaken. The bird thinks it's attacking a rival, but is in fact actually hammering away at its own reflected image. You may find that funny, but the truth is that when birds began to evolve tens of millions of years ago, there were no windows around for them to absorb into their experience and adapt accordingly. We, the window inventors, are to blame for their folly. This behavior is territorial and occurs during the breeding season when male birds, testosterone coursing through their bodies, stake out their patch of garden, attract a mate and then defend her from intruders and interlopers. A great many garden birds attack their own reflection at this time of year wherever they come across it in or close to the territory they are defending. As well as windows, they will also launch themselves at car wing mirrors, shiny hub caps and bumpers and even sun roofs. Although the bird will lose valuable energy fighting its own image, it comes to no harm and will eventually return to the important tasks of building the family nest, copulating with its partner and rearing its young.

HOW TO AVOID WINDOW FATALITIES

Windows cause the deaths of millions of birds every year, and the cleaner the window, the greater the threat they pose. On bright days, the glass reflects the world beyond and birds are fooled into flying straight at them. Big, tall French windows are the serial killers of the glass world. Many birds break their necks on collision and die, although some are simply stunned and manage to come round before they wake up in the mouth of the resident cat. One simple solution is to put a few stickers on the glass on the outside of the window. Images of birds, especially birds of prey, have proved to be a very effective deterrent.

Walking underwater

The dipper, a plump little bird with a white bib, walks along the bed of fast-flowing streams and small rivers turning over stones in search of food. It is the only bird that can do this. It stops itself floating to the surface by digging its toes into the bed of the stream. Its stubby wings are well adapted for swimming and it has its own built-in goggles that are activated underwater, as well as a large preening gland for oiling and waterproofing its feathers.

Why do we see so few dead birds?

Although millions of birds die every year in the US, it is very rare to come across a dead body, save for a pheasant in the road or a pigeon that has been ambushed by a sparrowhawk. A crucial link in the food chain, most small birds are eaten by mammals and other birds, explaining why many species produce so many offspring. Once they have finished with the flesh of the bird, scavengers and predators such as foxes, cats and rats will leave only the feathers behind and these will soon be scattered by the winds or swallowed up by the undergrowth. Sick birds, like many animals, retreat into secluded hideaways to recover and are unlikely to be found if they die there. A bird that does just drop dead will decompose very quickly as the insects get to work on its light body mass.

" The much abused and persecuted Red Wing Black Bird is found throughout North America, from the Atlantic to the Pacific; and it breeds more or less abundantly wherever found . . . Sometimes they appear as if driven about like an enormous black cloud carried before the wind, varying every moment in shape. Sometimes they rise suddenly from the fields with a noise like thunder, while the glittering of innumerable wings of the brightest vermillion, amid the black cloud, occasion a very striking effect. At times the whole congregated multitude will suddenly alight in some detached grove and commence one general concert, that can plainly be distinguished at the distance of more than two miles . . . In the grain growing states they gather in immense swarms and commit havoc, and although they are shot in great numbers, and though their ranks are thinned by the attacks of hawks, it seems to have but little effect upon the survivors. On the other hand, these Black Birds more than compensate the farmer for their mischief by the benefit they confer in the destruction of grub worms, caterpillars, and various kinds of larvae, the secret and deadly enemies of vegetation. It has been estimated the number of insects destroyed by these birds in a single season, in the United States, to be twelve thousand millions. "

FROM THE MAGAZINE *BIRDS*, PUBLISHED FEBRUARY 1897

~~~~~~~~

You cannot prevent the birds of sorrow from flying over your head, but you can prevent them from building nests in your hair.

CHINESE PROVERB

~~~~~~~~

Voles are just pissing in the wind

When you see a kestrel hovering at the side of a road or field, it is looking for its favorite food, the vole. How these birds of prey, up to 66 feet above the ground, manage to see the tiny rodents shuffling nervously beneath the undergrowth had never been satisfactorily explained – until recently. Yes, kestrels like all birds of prey have tremendous eyesight, but the suspicion was that there was more to it than that. Voles are seriously small and they spend most of their time under the cover of vegetation, only rarely emerging into the open. From time to time, vole populations suffer sudden and huge crashes, forcing kestrels to travel hundreds of miles to find new vole-rich territory. How do they find these new areas so quickly, before they die of starvation? In 1995, Finnish scientists at the University of Turku produced the surprising explanation: the birds can see the trail of urine that voles leave wherever they go. Voles urinate as they go, because they use the urine as a navigation aid and as a way of communicating with each other. The trails are visible in ultraviolet light, which kestrels can detect, a skill that enables them to scan large areas in a short time.

No nut too tough to crack

The five species of grosbeaks found across North America come in all manner of colors and shades, but they have one distinguishing feature in common: a massive, stubby bill. The name *grosbeak* actually means "great bill," and it has been designed for cracking open the shells of seeds. Like its Transatlantic cousin the hawfinch, or European grosbeak, the bills of these birds can wield a force of more than 110 pounds – almost 1,000 times their body weight – and can crack a cherry stone in under five seconds. In his 21-volume *Life Histories of North American Birds*, Arthur Cleveland Bent describes how he watched a male rose-breasted grosbeak teaching his offspring to put use his bill:

The father then started to show it how to break open sunflower seeds. Perching beside his offspring on a branch, he cracked a seed, broke the kernel into pieces, and fed it to the young bird. He then gave it a whole kernel. Next, he pretended to give the fledgling an uncracked whole seed, but held on to it and in due time cracked the seed and fed the young bird. [After a week of this], irritability on the part of the parent, which had been increasing, resulted in his jamming food into the mouth of the young bird, pecking its bill, and driving it away.

Why does the robin eat alone and the sparrow in a group?

The house sparrow lives off seeds and scraps, which are often found in patches, and it is a more efficient use of energy if a cluster of the birds seek out these food sources. The birds work as a team and when one strikes it lucky, the others arrive to join in the bonanza before they all move on in search of more. This group foraging is also common among many seabirds seeking shoals of fish. Its virtue is that between them the birds form a mobile information center, with each bird supplying and responding to the pooled information. Like the blackbird and the thrush, the robin is a solitary feeder owing to the fact that it eats mainly worms and insects from the ground. The last thing it wants to do when it plucks a nice fat earthworm from the soil is invite the neighbors round to share its catch.

Bird Brain

INSTINCT OR INTELLIGENCE?

How intelligent are birds?

A bird can't read a book or work out compound interest rates, but then again a man can't navigate his way from South Africa to the same nest site in New York every spring. If you lay the dissected brains of a human being and a bird alongside each other, a man in a long white coat (with a brain the size of Canada) will be able to point out why the intelligence of the two creatures is so different. The most highly developed part of man's brain is the cerebral cortex, the area for learning and remembering, explaining why man can write piano concertos and work out the theory of relativity. The most highly developed area in a bird is the cerebellum, which controls movement and coordination, explaining why a bird can weave in and out of a thousand branches at 30 mph in fading light without crashing.

> *Those little nimble musicians of the air that warble forth their curious ditties with which nature hath furnished them to the shame of art.*
>
> ENGLISH WRITER IZAAK WALTON
> (1593–1683)

The front part of the bird brain is smaller than a mammal's and the most important section of it is the diencephalon where genetically inherited information is retained. It is this area of the brain that informs, say, a young cuckoo, setting out by itself on its first migration, exactly where to go. Most birds fly the family nest as soon as they can fly, a matter of weeks in most species, whereas human young stay and learn from their parents for a very long period before making their own way in the world. Social birds, such as blue tits, will imitate their parents to a certain extent, but mostly they rely upon a combination of instinct, prompted by the genetic computer in their forebrain, and trial and error. If they eat a berry or an insect that makes them sick, they will know not to eat it again.

The learning capacity of birds is very limited – though crows and parrots, the most "intelligent" birds by human standards, might buttonhole you about that. They are among a handful of birds that can learn new tricks. Crows in Japanese cities drop walnuts in front of cars at traffic lights then sit on the overhead pylons and wait for an obliging wheel to break the shell open. A crow can also strip a stick of leaves and off-shoots and use it as a tool for digging out grubs. The song thrush works out that it can get at the flesh of a snail by dashing its shell against a rock. Sparrows are consistently inventive in their search for food, raiding spiders' webs for insects and even the grilles of cars where insects collect.

> *I never saw a wild thing sorry for itself. A small bird will drop frozen dead from a bough without ever having felt sorry for itself.*
>
> ENGLISH WRITER D. H. LAWRENCE
> (1885–1930)

Birds have very little consciousness: they don't reflect on the past, or project their thoughts into the future. They live in the now and are only interested in knowledge that helps them to survive. It may take tens of thousands of years for that information to sink in. But that doesn't make birds stupid. If they were stupid, they'd go and talk to a cat. Or start wars and put all their money in the stock exchange.

The Kingfisher

It was the Rainbow gave thee birth,
  And left thee all her lovely hues;
And, as her mother's name was Tears,
  So runs it in thy blood to choose
For haunts the lonely pools, and keep
In company with trees that weep.

Go you and, with such glorious hues,
  Live with proud Peacocks in green parks;
On lawns as smooth as shining glass,
  Let every feather show its marks;
Get thee on boughs and clap thy wings
Before the windows of proud kings.

Nay, lovely Bird, thou art not vain;
  Thou hast no proud ambitious mind;
I also love a quiet place
  That's green, away from all mankind;
A lonely pool, and let a tree
Sigh with her bosom over me.

W. H. DAVIES

How and why does a starling mimic the ring of my cell phone?

An African gray parrot named Alex achieved minor celebrity for having built up a vocabulary of 800 words during his long life, but it's not just fancy captive birds that can learn the sounds created by human beings and their machines. A number of wild birds are equally adept at mimicry, including the lyrebirds and bower-birds of Australasia and the mockingbirds of the Americas. Even the humble blackbird and starling hopping about in your garden can put the world's best impersonators to shame with the accuracy of their sound representation. If you exposed them to the whining sound long enough, all these birds could imitate the sound of disappointed golfers, fishermen and Cleveland Indian fans to perfection. You may well have heard the ring of a cell phone, the wail of an ambulance siren or the jaunty tune of a man whistling not realizing that it was in fact a small bird sitting on a nearby roof running through its latest repertoire. Not, by any means, that all blackbirds and starlings spend their days running through a catalog of impressions, but if they hear certain sounds for long enough, then eventually they will start to repeat them.

Songbirds learn their songs from the adults around them, mainly from the males, who do far more vocalizing than the females. If a bird is constantly exposed to the song of a different species then it will learn its neighbor's repertoire too. And if that bird happens to live next to a house or office where it can hear the constant trill of a telephone, then eventually it will learn to imitate that sound as well. Ornithologists suspect that birds mimic sounds for the same reason that they sing their lungs out in spring: to make themselves more attractive to a female and to intimidate any rivals at the start of the breeding season. There's nothing a female bird likes more than to be serenaded by a desperate male banging out the sound of a police siren or a jackhammer from the treetops.

> The common cormorant or shag
> Lays eggs inside a paper bag
> The reason you will see no doubt
> It is to keep the lightning out
> But what these unobservant birds
> Have never noticed is that herds
> Of wandering bears may come with buns
> And steal the bags to hold the crumbs.
>
> **ENGLISH NOVELIST CHRISTOPHER ISHERWOOD (1904–86)**

Mozart-whistling starling

The great Austrian composer Mozart bought a starling from a pet store in 1784 after hearing it whistle the beginning of the last movement of his Piano Concerto No.17 in G major, K453. Although the silly bird sang G sharp instead of G natural, Mozart was still mightily impressed and took him home, jotting the date, price and the notes the bird was singing into an expenses book. When the bird died, three years later, Mozart buried it in his garden and recited a poem he wrote to mark the solemn occasion.

~ ~ ~ ~ ~

A bird does not sing because it has an answer. It sings because it has a song.

CHINESE PROVERB

~ ~ ~ ~ ~

I'd teach a starling how to speak and sing,
Till every word and note with truth should ring,
With all the skill my lips and tongue impart,
With all the warmth and passion of my heart.
Then let him brightly sing it through her windowpane:
Thine is my heart, Thine is my heart,
And shall forever, forever so remain!

GERMAN POET WILHELM MÜLLER (1794–1827), FROM *DIE SCHÖNE MÜLLERIN* (*THE BEAUTIFUL MILL GIRL*), A POEM TURNED INTO A WELL-KNOWN SONG CYCLE BY AUSTRIAN COMPOSER FRANZ SCHUBERT

Collective nouns of some common birds

A murder of crows
A kettle of hawks
A charm of hummingbirds
An exaltation of larks
A parliament of
    owls/rooks
A bevy of quail
An unkindness of ravens

A wisp of snipe
A chatter of starlings
A pitying of turtledoves
A knob of widgeons
A plump of wildfowl
A fall of woodcocks
A herd of wrens

Hollywood crows

Alfred Hitchcock used over 600 real birds alongside a number of stuffed and mechanical ones in the filming of his classic 1963 horror film *The Birds*. Crows, seagulls, hawks, ravens, eagles, finches and starlings were trained for several months to become feathered actors, to add some terrifying realism to the scenes. The crows were the stars of the show, according to trainer Ray Berwick who taught his favorite one, Nosey, to fetch his car keys and even to put a cigarette in his mouth and light it for him. "I'm amazed at the reasoning power of the crow," Berwick told *Time* magazine during filming in the Hollywood studio, where the set was contained within a giant polythene bag to stop the birds crashing into the lights and equipment. "Crows are the chimpanzees of birds. The hardest to train and catch are the hawks and eagles. You could teach them to hunt and kill, but they know it already. But you can't teach them any tricks." Grips coaxed the birds back and forth across the set with food, and blasts of air were used to send the birds into a flurry of wild flapping. In some scenes the actors smeared their hands and faces with raw hamburger and waited for the birds to peck them. "Birds make excellent heavies," Hitchcock told *Time*. "After all, they've been put in cages, shot at, and shoved into ovens for centuries. It's only natural they should fight back. Many people are terrified of them. Once the picture is released, it may do wonders for cat sales and the scarecrow market."

A wise old owl sat on an oak;
The more he saw the less he spoke;
The less he spoke the more he heard;
Why aren't we like that wise old bird?

ANONYMOUS

❝ Many amateurs still think that when birds sing and hop around, they are being merry and affectionate. They are not, of course; they are being aggressive and demanding the price of a cup of coffee. As, however, human beings are soft at heart and in the head, I suppose we shall go on regarding this thing as a much loved garden bird, even when it beats on the window with its beak and tells you to get that goddam food on the bird table or else. ❞

BRITISH JOURNALIST MILES KINGTON (1941–2008)

How did the blue tit craze of opening milk bottles catch on so fast?

Foil-topped milk bottles, delivered to Britain's doorsteps, were introduced in the 1920s and almost immediately blue tits started pecking through the lids to get to the cream on top, leaving ornithologists up and down Britain open-mouthed in astonishment. Groups of these ever-restless and inquisitive birds even started following milkmen on their rounds, while others would sit near a doorstep waiting for the daily delivery to which they had become accustomed. The trend quickly spread through the entire tit population, baffling birdwatchers, scientists and milkmen in equal measure. The big question was: given that most tits only lived a year or so, how on earth did they manage to pass on the good news to their family and friends? Some thought the knowledge was passed through the genes, but even the pioneers of genetic science knew that the milk-top phenomenon was spreading way too fast for evolution to have absorbed the new trick and passed it on to the next generation. Proper research soon showed that the birds were learning the knack through a combination of their own experiments and the sight of older birds doing it. The point was proved by observation of robins' behavior: occasionally a robin was also seen to peck through the foil, but the habit never caught on among the wider robin population because, the eggheads quickly worked out, the robin feeds alone, unobserved by its young. For the record, blue tits prefer full-fat milk to skimmed.

❝ Here I met with one of the most extraordinary phenomena that I ever saw, or heard of: – Mr. Sellers has in his yard a large Newfoundland dog, and an old raven. These have fallen deeply in love with each other, and never desire to be apart. The bird has learned the bark of the dog, so that few can distinguish them. She is inconsolable when he goes out; and, if he stays out a day or two, she will get up all the bones and scraps she can, and hoard them up for him till he comes back. ❞

JOHN WESLEY (1703–91)

~ ~ ~ ~ ~

Western man has no need of more superiority over nature whether outside or inside. He has both in an almost devilish perfection. What he lacks is conscious recognition of his inferiority to the nature around and within him. He must learn that he may not do exactly as he wills. If he does not learn this, his own nature will destroy him.

CARL JUNG (1875–1961)

~ ~ ~ ~ ~

Not so clever now, are we?

The Greek poet Aeschylus is supposed to have died when an eagle, mistaking his bald head for a rock on which it could crack open its supper, dropped a tortoise on him from a great height.

Some Geese

Every child who has the use
Of his senses knows a goose.
See them underneath the tree
Gather round the goose-girl's knee,
While she reads them by the hour
From the works of Schopenhauer.

How patiently the geese attend!
But do they really comprehend
What Schopenhauer's driving at?
Oh, not at all; but what of that?
Neither do I; neither does she;
And, for that matter, nor does he.

OLIVER HERFORD

The Battle to Survive

HOW BIRDS ARE COPING IN A DAMAGED WORLD

Why is there so much doom and gloom about the future of the world's wildlife?

Wildlife habitats are fragile, miniature ecosystems and the food chains sustaining animals that live in them are delicate, neatly balanced structures. Both are highly vulnerable to change – and the change to the natural world in the course of the Industrial Age has been phenomenal, especially during the first half of the twentieth century. Most species of birds, mammals, insects and fish are struggling to come to terms with the momentous upheaval to the environment; many are threatened with extinction, many more are endangered. For millions of years, nature's creatures had nothing but themselves to fret about and even after man entered the scene in significant numbers a few thousand years ago, the natural world changed very little. But in the space of two hundred years or so man has caused an astonishing amount of havoc to the world he shares with other creatures, both deliberately and unwittingly. The situation has become so critical that the vast majority of scientists and other experts fear that, unless we take radical action and take it very, very soon, then nature – being a giant, interconnecting, interdependent network – will start to implode, rapidly disappearing into a vortex of decline and destruction.

As far back as 1970, U Thant, then Secretary-General of the United Nations, said in a speech:

"As we watch the sun go down, evening after evening, through the smog across the poisoned waters of our native earth, we must ask ourselves seriously whether we really wish some future universal historian on another planet to say about us: 'With all their genius and with all their skill, they ran out of foresight and air and food and water and ideas,' or 'They went on playing politics until their world collapsed around them.'"

And today, the environment is in an even more perilous state than it was 40 years ago . . .

The alarming state of American birds

Almost a third of America's 800 bird species are endangered, threatened, or in sharp decline due to habitat loss, invasive species, environmental degradation and other threats, according to a study issued in 2009. Analyzing changes in the bird population's over the past 40 years, "The State of the Birds" report is the most authoritative survey of American bird life ever undertaken and includes a wealth of evidence from government agencies, conservation organizations and citizen volunteer schemes. Sixty-seven US bird species are federally listed as endangered or threatened while 184 species are designated as birds of concern. Grassland birds have become the biggest cause for concern with their numbers down 40 percent, mainly as a result of the relentless destruction of their habitat. Birds depending on coastal waters declined by 39 percent, arid land species were down by 30 percent and, although forest birds have fared better overall than birds in other habitats, many species are threatened by suburban sprawl, logging, wildfires, pests and disease. Other threats to bird numbers include pesticides, predation by cats and collisions with windows, towers and buildings.

How many birds have become extinct in modern times?

The rate of extinction has increased enormously since the late fifteenth century when European countries first began exploring and colonizing the world. A great deal of damage had already been done by Polynesians to ever-vulnerable island species in the Pacific, but the arrival in the New World of Europeans, with their guns and their animals, took the devastation to a new level. The very latest research suggests that the world has lost around 500 species of bird since the start of the sixteenth century (rather than between 100 and 200 as had been thought for many years). That's an average of one species per year, a rate 100 times greater than the natural cycle that had existed for tens of millions of years up until then. Before the rise of man, approximately one bird species per century disappeared from the world. We have managed to kill off hundreds in a blink of history's eye and unless drastic action is taken in the next few years, the prospects for birds in the twenty-first century are looking even grimmer. A slew of recent reports by authoritative bodies suggest that between 10 and 20 percent of bird species will disappear in the next 100 years as climate change and environmental degradation tighten their grip on the planet.

> I have very little to say regarding this bird [Haast's Eagle, now extinct] as I have only seen two of them, and being pushed with hunger, I ate the pair of them. Under the circumstances I would have eaten the last of the dodo. It is all very well for science, lifting up its hands in horror, at what I once heard called gluttony, but let science tramp through the Westland bush or swamps [of New Zealand], for two or three days without food, and find out what hunger is. Besides at the time, which was many years ago, I was not aware that it was an almost extinct bird. Had I known so, I would at least have skinned it and kept the head and feet.
>
> **EXPLORER CHARLES EDWARD DOUGLAS (1840–1916)**

An ill wind blowing through the prairies

Of all the grim prognoses of America's troubled habitats to emerge from the 2009 "State of the Birds" report, perhaps the most alarming was the news from the nation's once abundant prairies. Just under half of the 46 grassland-breeding birds have become a species of concern, including 8 of 12 sparrow species. Four are on the dreaded federal list of endangered species and 55 percent are showing significant declines.

Native grasslands once spread right across the United States from Canada to Mexico and west from Ohio to the Rocky Mountains, a vast home not just for millions of buffalo but also a wide variety of bird species including ducks, grouse, hawks and songbirds. It is little wonder, however, that those birds are struggling when you learn that 97 percent of the tallgrass prairie that existed in the early nineteenth century has been lost to farming while short- and midgrass prairies continue to be converted to agriculture today. The mechanization and intensification of agriculture has wreaked havoc among grassland birds and other wildlife groups around the world. The creation of larger fields has removed grassy edges, hedgerows, copses, ponds, plants and insects – in short, all the places birds need to live and forage. Much pastureland is also overgrazed and either burned too often or at the wrong time of year. Scientists also forecast that global warming will increase drought conditions in grassland areas, meaning even fewer food sources for birds.

Some of the nation's best-known birds are struggling. Forty years ago, for instance, there were 24 million eastern meadowlarks; today there are less than 7 million. In the same period, northern bobwhite numbers have plummeted from over 30 million to just over 5 million. (If that still sounds like a lot of birds, then consider that the passenger pigeon went from being the world's most populous bird to global extinction in less than a century.)

The good news is that there are easy and inexpensive ways of haying, mowing, grazing and burning that would arrest the steep decline in many grassland bird numbers. Only our political initiative and a modest amount of resources are needed to reverse the trend.

What Americans cannot control are the changing habitats over their borders. A significant number of birds that breed in the United States, for example, spend the winter in the Chihuahuan Desert grasslands of Mexico, but in the past few years more than a million acres of that area have been converted to agriculture. Other species, such as the bobolink, American golden-plover and Swainson's hawk fly to South America where grasslands are also being taken over by the farming industry.

20 Common North American Birds with the Greatest Population Declines Since 1967

Northern bobwhite

Evening grosbeak

Northern pintail

Greater scaup

Boreal chickadee

Eastern meadowlark

Common tern

Loggerhead shrike

Field sparrow

Grasshopper sparrow

Snow bunting

Black-throated sparrow

Lark sparrow

Common grackle

American bittern

Rufous hummingbird

Whip-poor-will

Horned lark

Little blue heron

Ruffed grouse

Grassland species federally listed as endangered

Aplomado falcon

Greater prairie-chicken

Northern bobwhite

Grasshopper sparrow

America's top 10 most endangered birds

Ivory-billed woodpecker

California condor

Whooping crane

Gunnison sage-grouse

Kirtland's warbler

Piping plover

Florida scrub-jay

Ashy storm petrel

Golden-cheeked warbler

Kittlitz's murrelet

Seven ways to help birds

1. Attract birds to your yard by growing native plants that provide food and nesting sites.

2. Provide bird food and clean water.

3. Put out birdhouses to encourage nesting.

4. Prevent window collisions by putting stickers and silhouettes on the clear glass.

5. Follow the National Audubon Society's initiative by buying shade-grown, organic, pesticide-free coffee that creates an important winter habitat for migratory songbirds.

6. Take part in national projects, like the Christmas Bird Count and the Great Backyard Bird Count, to help increase our knowledge of bird numbers.

7. Keep cats indoors.

Ivory-billed woodpecker: the gradual extinction of hope

The fate of the ivory-billed woodpecker has become a cause célèbre among American conservationists who have been searching for it high and low in the woodlands of Arkansas in recent years. Once common across the southeastern United States, the crow-size bird was thought to have become extinct in the 1940s after losing much of its bottom-land forest habitat to agriculture, logging and water diversion. But in 2004, ornithologists in the Cache River and White River national wildlife refuges reported a sighting and made a sound recording of its knocking. Despite the deployment of a federal recovery team and the investment of $10 million in funds and donations, subsequent efforts to confirm the existence of the world's third largest woodpecker (with its distinctive bold black and white plumage) have so far yielded only frowns of disappointment from the hundreds of people who have set out to find it. Skeptics have questioned the wisdom in spending so much time, effort and money in hunting for a bird that in all probability died out decades ago, but many refuse to see their hopes follow the woodpecker, nicknamed the "Lord God Bird," into extinction.

Slaughter in the bird sanctuary

Over 50 percent of New Zealand's native birds have become extinct since the first human settlers set foot on the islands somewhere around AD 900. Until then, the country was a giant bird sanctuary with no mammals there except for bats, which don't prey on birds. Without any predators to harass them, many birds had a perfect evolutionary excuse for dropping their guard. Why bother going to the energy-sapping effort of flying when there's nothing to fly away from and all the food and shelter necessary is right there on the forest floor? Many birds became flightless and took to building their nests on the ground. When the first Polynesians stepped out of their canoes and came ashore, they would have been delighted to see thousands

North American bird species with large sample sizes undergoing the greatest population declines from 1966 to 2003

1.	Rusty blackbird	−97.9%	2,000,000
2.	Henslow's sparrow	−96.4%	79,000
3.	Common tern	−90.6%	1,400,000
4.	Verdin	−85.6%	8,900,000
5.	Sprague's pipit	−83.8%	870,000
6.	Pinyon jay	−82.5%	4,100,000
7.	Short-eared owl	−80.3%	2,400,000
8.	Cerulean warbler	−79.6%	560,000
9.	Black-throated sparrow	−79.6%	27,000,000
10.	Loggerhead shrike	−77.1%	4,200,000

of giant moa birds, roaming the open plains and forests. The moa was a roast meal waiting to happen and by 1700 there were none left. They had all been killed, cooked, consumed and crapped into the undergrowth. Life got even worse for New Zealand's bird kingdom when the white man turned up with his guns, his rats, his cats and his eagerness to chop down the forests and plow the land to create fields for his crops and his cattle.

New species still out there

Every year or so the odd new species of bird is found in some dark corner of a distant forest, generally in the more remote areas of South America but also in other tropical regions such as southeast Asia (mainly Indonesia) and central Africa. The thrill of discovery, however, is dampened by the fact that the birds are invariably put straight on to the endangered species list.

The sad tale of the penguin of the north

Although it may well be joined by a number of others in the coming decades, so far the flightless great auk is the only British bird to have suffered the fate of global extinction. This large seabird that looked like a penguin crossed with a razorbill was once a common sight on the northern shores of the UK before people began clubbing, strangling and shooting it into oblivion. At first it was slaughtered for food, for its fat and for use as commercial fishing bait, but toward the end of its existence it was for its feathers and eggs that it was relentlessly harassed and finally exterminated. The feathers were used in fashion while the increasingly rare eggs found their way into collectors' display cabinets. The last great auk in the British Isles was killed on the island of St. Kilda, off Scotland's west coast, in the summer of 1840. The last population of the great auk, which used to be found throughout the North Atlantic and was also called "penguin" or "gairfowl," lived on a volcanic island off southern Iceland, known as Geirfuglasker or "Great Auk Rock." On this island fortified by sheer cliffs all the way round, the birds were relatively safe from man's meddling and might well have survived for centuries longer. But in 1830, there was a volcanic episode under the sea and the island disappeared in an avalanche of tumbling rock, boiling water and clouds of steam. Was there nowhere safe on the planet for this beleaguered, defenseless bird? The great auk was a strong swimmer and the survivors of the volcanic catastrophe took to the water and found sanctuary on the nearby island of Eldey. Relief, however, was only temporary as the hunters were quick to locate and corner their prey. On June 3, 1844 the last pair was strangled to death and their egg crushed under the heel of a heavy boot.

The Victorian author Charles Kingsley was puzzled and upset by the extinction of the auk. He wrote about its demise in his 1863 children's book *The Water-Babies*:

> Once we were a great nation, and spread over all the Northern Isles. But men shot us so, and knocked us on the head, and took our eggs – why, if you will believe it, they say that on the coast of Labrador the sailors used to lay a plank from the rock on board the thing called their ship, and drive us along the plank by hundreds, till we tumbled down into the ship's waist in heaps; and then, I suppose, they ate us, the nasty fellows! Well – but – what was I saying? At last, there were none of us left, except on the old Gairfowlskerry, just off the Iceland coast, up which no man could climb. Even there we had no peace; for

one day, when I was quite a young girl, the land rocked, and the sea boiled, and the sky grew dark, and all the air was filled with smoke and dust, and down tumbled the old Gair-fowlskerry into the sea. The dovekies and marrocks, of course, all flew away; but we were too proud to do that. Some of us were dashed to pieces, and some drowned; and those who were left got away to Eldey, and the dovekies tell me they are all dead now, and that another Gairfowlskerry has risen out of the sea close to the old one, but that it is such a poor flat place that it is not safe to live on: and so here I am left alone.

How many birds are killed by cats every year?

Scientists estimate that each year America's 80 million domestic cats kill hundreds of millions of birds, including common species such as the cardinal, blue jay and robin as well as endangered ones such as the piping plover and Florida scrub-jay. North America is also plagued by tens of millions of stray and feral cats that prey upon the wild bird population. Cats are the most widespread and destructive predator on the planet and are now considered to be the second biggest cause of declining global bird numbers behind loss of habitat. Cats also kill billions of small mammals, such as field mice and shrews, putting them in direct competition with many birds of prey.

Alarming bird facts

- One in eight of the world's birds – 1,226 species in total – face extinction. Of those, 190 are Critically Endangered.

- Farmland birds in Europe have declined by 34 percent since 1966.

- 67 percent of globally threatened birds on ocean islands are endangered by alien invasive species.

- Agricultural expansion and intensification threaten 50 percent of Important Bird Areas in Africa.

- 43 percent of Africa's Important Bird Areas have no legal recognition or protection.

- 64 percent of globally threatened birds, most of them in the tropics, are threatened by unsustainable forestry.

- Conservation investment is over 20 times higher in developed than developing countries.

(Birdlife International and the International Union for the Conservation of Nature)

It is a melancholy reflection, that, from man, downwards, to the smallest living creature, all are found to prey upon and devour each other. The philosophic mind, however, sees this waste of animal life again and again repaired by fresh stores, ever ready to supply the void, and the great work of generation and destruction perpetually going on, and to this dispensation of an all-wise Providence, so interesting to humanity, bows in awful silence.

THOMAS BEWICK (1753–1828)

President Teddy Roosevelt was a key figure in the early years of the conservation movement, forcing through a raft of laws to protect birds in the United States during his eight-year term of office at the start of the twentieth century. He was also responsible for the establishment of 53 Federal Wildlife Refuges across the country, as well as 18 areas of special interest and 40 million acres of national forests. In his earlier incarnation as governor of New York, he forced the closure of factories trading in bird feathers.

Is it a bird? Is it a plane?

The whooping crane, like the California condor, has been the focus of concerted and imaginative efforts by American conservationists to boost its numbers and drag it back from the edge of oblivion. This graceful white bird with the long black bill once bred in large numbers across the central prairies of the northern United States and Canada, migrating south to winter in northern Mexico, the Texas Gulf coast and a small stretch of the Atlantic coast. From the late nineteenth century, its numbers began to fall sharply due to hunting, collecting and loss of habitat. By World War II, there were only about 15 of America's tallest bird left in the wild. Today, their numbers have risen to almost 400, thanks in part to the use of open-cockpit ultra-light aircrafts leading dozens of the birds bred in captivity on an annual migration between Necedah National Wildlife Refuge in Wisconsin and Chassahowitzka National Wildlife Refuge in Florida.

Newsflash: the dodo is still extinct

The dodo was the first recorded of the many bird species killed off by man. Found only on the previously uninhabited island of Mauritius in the Indian Ocean, the dodo had, over time, become flightless because there were no land-based predators from which it needed to flee into the air. For tens of millions of years the dodos built their nests on the ground and happily waddled around their island paradise munching on fruit, rearing their young and minding their own business. And then man came ashore. After its discovery by the

Portuguese in 1598, sailors started to use Mauritius as a port of call to stock up on food and water and carry out repairs on their ships. Plump, fleshy birds, bigger than turkeys, that couldn't fly away were easy prey for man, his dogs and his egg-eating pigs and monkeys. In 1681, less than a century after the species encountered its first human being, the last dodo on earth was clubbed to death by a hungry sailor. All that remains of the dodo today is a head and foot at Oxford University, a foot in London's British Museum, a head in Copenhagen, plus a few bones scattered around museums in Europe and the United States.

Return flight for the California condor

The California condor, the largest bird in North America, remains one of the most endangered birds in the United States, but its remarkable recovery from the very brink of extinction has given hope to conservation causes around the world.

Weighing over 18 pounds and with a wingspan of more than 9 feet, the condor was once a common sight in the skies above Arizona, Utah, Montana, Colorado, Wyoming, California, Idaho and Oregon but, persecuted and poisoned by man for decades, it became extinct in the wild in 1987, when the last six of these giant, prehistoric-looking scavengers were captured and put into a captive-breeding program. The birds, which feed on large mammal carcasses, have been slowly reintroduced and their population has risen steadily to reach about 160 by 2008 with a further 140 in captivity.

The condor's only natural predator is man, and the only threats to its survival are man-made. Its fate still hangs in the balance because a pair can only produce one chick a year, and human activities continue to pose grave threats. Shooting, collisions with power lines and poisoning from coyote-control programs have killed dozens of the birds since their reintroduction, but the main threat is lead poisoning from eating carcasses that have been shot with bullets containing the toxic metal. The scarcity of food has also been a major factor behind the bird's decline: in prehistoric times, mammoths, camels, elephant-size mastodons and massive herds of buffalo roamed the American landscape and provided rich pickings for these huge vultures, but today the birds will be lucky to find anything larger than a deer carcass.

Trouble in paradise

Hawaii has earned itself the unwanted reputation as the "extinction capital of the world" after losing dozens of its birds to oblivion following the arrival first of Polynesians in the fourth century and then Europeans in the late eighteenth. Like all island ecosystems, those of the Hawaiian archipelago have proven to be drastically vulnerable to invasive species of animals and plants. The once pristine environments of the islands, thousands of miles from a continental landmass, provided the perfect habitat for hundreds of species to evolve over millions of years. But in the blink of history's eyes many of them have gone the way of the dodo, never to walk the planet, fish its waters or fly its skies ever again.

It is thought that more than 71 species have become extinct on Hawaii since man first pulled ashore his canoes and set about colonizing the Pacific chain. One-third of all US listed bird species are found in Hawaii, and there are fears that a great number of them may soon follow many of their former cohabitants to extinction. Thirty-one are federally listed as threatened or endangered – and 10 of these have not been seen for more than 40 years and, in all probability, are extinct.

After Captain Cook and his crew became the first Europeans to reach Hawaii in January 1778, the introduction of pigs, sheep, horses, cattle, cats, dogs and rodents – followed shortly afterward by nonnative plant species – wreaked havoc with the local flora and fauna. The habitat of many native species was overrun and many animals and birds were forced higher into the native forest into ever smaller areas, leading inevitably to a crash in population numbers. The declines continue today and the calls by conservationists for radical remedial action are growing louder and louder as the songs and calls of the forests and coastlines fall quieter and quieter. In 2007, the American Bird Conservancy (ABC) declared that the forests of Hawaii were the most threatened bird habitat in the United States.

Birds and bulldozers

Birds have learned to live in every habitat on earth, from the frozen ice caps of the polar regions to the scorching heat of the desert, from mountain ranges to wetlands, coastlines, scrub, cities and parks. But three quarters of the world's 10,000 bird species live in the forests,

Hawaii's 10 most endangered birds

1. Hawaiian crow ('Alala) – Extinct in the wild; 50 in captivity
2. Millerbird – 30 to 730
3. Puaiohi (small Kaua'i thrush) – 200 to 300
4. Laysan duck – 375 to 500
5. Maui parrotbill – 500
6. 'Akiapola'au – 1,163
7. 'Akikiki – 1,472
8. Nihoa finch – 1,500 to 3,200
9. Koloa (Hawaiian duck) – 2,200 to 2,525
10. 'Akohekohe (crested honeycreeper) – 3,750 to 3,800

List compiled by the Audubon Society with population estimates based on surveys by biologists of the US Fish and Wildlife Service, US Geological Survey, the USDA Forest Service, the Department of Fish and Wildlife and their partners.

especially the humid, damp forests of the tropics that cover just 5 percent of the world's land surface. As the rain forests recoil at the advance of the bulldozer, the number of species and the number of individual birds shrink in proportion; and the rate of extinction is set to accelerate sharply because many tropical species have very small breeding areas.

Let us prey

One tenth of the world's bird species are congregatory, including a great number of waterbirds and migrants, gathering together into large, spectacular colonies to nest, breed, feed, roost or migrate. Living in a colony has many advantages, including greater safety from predators and sharing information about food sources, but it also makes these species extremely vulnerable to environmental

Top 10 most frequently reported birds

1. Northern cardinal

2. Mourning dove

3. Dark-eyed junco

4. American goldfinch

5. Downy woodpecker

6. Blue jay

7. House finch

8. Tufted titmouse

9. American crow

10. Black-capped chickadee

Reported in the 2009 Great Backyard Bird Count, a joint project of the Cornell Lab of Ornithology and the National Audubon Society. During the annual four-day event, the continent's bird lovers count birds to create a real-time snapshot of bird concentrations.

degradation, especially when large numbers of birds make use of just a few important sites. Indeed, some 20 percent of these species are categorized as "globally threatened."

Why we should all be alarmed by the recent sharp decline in bird populations

Like canaries down a mine alerting miners of old to a gas leak, the birds of today are sending out messages of foreboding about our poisoned, damaged world. Birds, as a whole group, are more sensitive to changes in their environment than other animals, so when they start falling off perches we should all be troubled. They are in the forward-most trench of nature's resistance against the relentless attrition of environmental degradation. Our birds are nature's early warning system and the scientists are telling us that if we don't start acting on their distress signals, it won't be long before the rest of the animal world is overrun as well. The populations of many species are declining rapidly because habitats are being destroyed or undermined, food sources are disappearing and, tricked by the increasingly weird and erratic weather, the birds' migration and breeding patterns are changing. In short, birds are confused and under stress. Just because you can hear your robins, blue tits and sparrows chirping away happily in the garden every morning, don't be fooled into thinking that all is well in "birdworld."

The impact of global warming has already started to work its sinister, insidious magic on migratory birds. Summer visitors to Britain are arriving in their breeding areas two to three weeks earlier than thirty years ago and as winters become even milder and spring arrives earlier and earlier, the birds will be fooled into setting off earlier and arriving at their summer residences before their food sources are ready. Those that winter in sub-Saharan Africa are likely to experience mounting problems as conditions get hotter and drier and the boundaries of the desert creep ever outwards. As the planet heats up, the ice retreats and the snowcaps melt, Arctic and montane species become ever more vulnerable. For cold-weather British birds such as the ptarmigan and the snow bunting, the future looks especially bleak. Enjoy them while they last because the ornithologists tell us they are likely to disappear in under a generation. Warmer seas and overfishing are having a devastating effect on marine stocks, which in turn is having a domino effect on seabird populations.

> My left arm ached from lifting my gun, my shoulder from the recoil, and I was deaf and stunned from the banging . . . When in the late afternoon the carnage stopped almost 4,000 pheasants had been killed. The bright limp carcasses were laid out in rows of 100; the whole place was littered with feathers and spent cartridges.

Edward VIII, then Prince of Wales, on a shooting party on the Buckinghamshire estate of Lord Burnham in 1913. His father, George V, suggested that the party had "perhaps gone too far."

How did the world's most abundant bird become extinct within 100 years?

In 1813 a flock of over a billion passenger pigeons measuring 300 miles long and three miles wide took four days to pass overhead, darkening the skies like a giant eclipse as it made its way across the United States. It is estimated that there were five billion passenger pigeons in North America at this time. By the start of World War I, when man turned his talents for mass killing onto himself, not a single bird of the species was left. The natural enemies of the passenger pigeon were hawks, owls, weasels, skunks and tree snakes, but their combined threat was as nothing compared to the greed and cruelty of man.

The birds were a good source of cheap meat for slaves and the poor. Settlers, heading further and further west, began slaughtering the long-tailed birds in their millions and selling them in city markets. After a gradual decline, their numbers collapsed between 1870 and 1890. Ornithologist and artist John James Audubon recorded how three million pigeons were sold by a single market hunter in the year 1878. Recent studies suggest that loss of habitat, caused by settlers clearing the land, was also a significant factor in the birds' decline. The settlers were extraordinarily inventive in the ways they found to exterminate the pigeons, many using giant nets to trap them before killing them by crushing their skulls with their thumbs.

On September 1, 1914, the bird became officially extinct when Martha, the last known survivor of the species, died in the Cincinnati Zoo. Martha, named after the wife of former President George Washington, was preserved in a block of ice and sent to the Smithsonian Institution where she was stuffed and mounted on a perch. In Wyalusing State Park in Wisconsin, a monument to the passenger pigeon reads: "This species became extinct through the avarice and thoughtlessness of man." But its rapid and dramatic disappearance was not all in vain as it drew attention to the issue of man's relationship with the natural world, and provided a huge spur to the fledgling conservation movement.

Wetland birds soar to new heights

The number of America's wetland birds has soared 60 percent in four decades, reversing decades of decline, thanks in large part to the inspirational efforts of conservationists, who have restored or sustained millions of acres of precious habitat. More than half of the nation's original wetlands have been drained or converted to other uses, leading to a collapse in the populations of the birds living there by the late 1960s, but well-run, generously funded and determined management projects, regionally coordinated across the United States, Canada and Mexico, have brought about one of the great successes in the history of the conservation movement.

Thirty-nine species of hunted waterfowl have increased by more than 100 percent during the past 40 years. Wetlands management, seen as a model for projects in other habitats, has also sparked a significant recovery in populations of other birds, including American white pelican, sandhill crane, black-necked tilt, osprey and kingfishers. Colonial-nesting wading birds, such as egrets, herons, and white ibis, are also making a strong comeback after the devastations wrought by the feather trade and hunting in the early twentieth century.

The Darkling Thrush

I leant upon a coppice gate
    When Frost was spectre-gray,
And Winter's dregs made desolate
    The weakening eye of day.

The tangled bine-stems scored the sky
  Like strings of broken lyres,
And all mankind that haunted nigh
  Had sought their household fires.

The land's sharp features seemed to be
  The Century's corpse outleant,
His crypt the cloudy canopy,
  The wind his death-lament.
The ancient pulse of germ and birth
  Was shrunken hard and dry,
And every spirit upon earth
  Seemed fervourless as I.

At once a voice arose among
  The bleak twigs overhead
In a full-hearted evensong
  Of joy illimited;
An aged thrush, frail, gaunt, and small,
  In blast-beruffled plume,
Had chosen thus to fling his soul
  Upon the growing gloom.

So little cause for carolings
  Of such ecstatic sound
Was written on terrestrial things
  Afar or nigh around,
That I could think there trembled through
  His happy good-night air
Some blessed Hope, whereof he knew
  And I was unaware.

ENGLISH NOVELIST AND POET THOMAS HARDY (1840–1928)

Written on the eve of the new century and published in the *Times* on New Year's Day, 1901, "The Darkling Thrush" captures the ambivalent feelings people had about the new modern epoch they were entering, leaving behind the certainties of the Victorian Age.

The troubled history of the peregrine falcon

A peregrine falcon swooping at full pelt to kill its prey in midair is one of nature's great spectacles, but it is a fairly rare sight these days. The peregrine may well be the fastest creature on the planet, clocking 180 mph as it swoops to conquer, and one of the most adaptable, but it has never been speedy or wily enough to escape the attentions of human beings. Prized for its falconry skills for centuries, this powerful, usually solitary bird has endured a dreadful 100 years or so in which it has been driven to the brink of extinction in North America and Europe.

Found on every continent in all manner of habitats, from steeping mountains to flat coastal plains, from tropical forests to semi-desert and scrub, the peregrine has proved to be one of the world's most successful species – until very recently. In the first half of the twentieth century it was persecuted by gamekeepers and landowners worried about their stocks of game birds. During World War II, thousands were killed in Britain to protect homing pigeons that were carrying important military messages from mainland Europe, but its numbers had recovered by 1955 after new legislation outlawed its killing.

Soon afterward, the population on both sides of the Atlantic began to plummet as fast as the bird itself takes its prey, crashing altogether in areas where it fed off birds on agricultural land. It was exterminated in land east of the Mississippi and southern Canada, while populations shriveled in the north and west of the United States. Numbers of other birds of prey, including golden and bald eagles, began to tumble as well and the causes of the dramatic decline remained a mystery until research scientists discovered that new agricultural pesticides were to blame.

Organochloride chemicals were moving up the food chain, causing the shells of the birds' eggs to become thinner so that they would break when incubated by the adult. Thanks to a ban on the harmful pesticides and the efforts of conservationists, the situation has improved significantly and peregrine numbers have climbed. Although it is not as common a sight in the United States as it once was, its numbers have recovered enough for it to be removed from the endangered species list in 1999.

If you go down to the woods today, you're in for a bad surprise . . .

They haven't quite reached the point where British bird lovers are more likely to find a teddy bears' picnic in their local woods than catch a glimpse or song of some of their previously common woodland birds, but ornithologists have been astounded to discover that their numbers have been dropping in recent years. Worse still, they don't understand why, and many fear that the problem is not a local British issue, but a global phenomenon with dire implications for hundreds of migratory birds.

Between 1994 and 2007, nightingale numbers in Britain were down by 60 percent, spotted flycatchers by 59 percent, willow tits by 77 percent, pied flycatchers by 54 percent and wood warblers by 67 percent, while the lesser spotted woodpecker has declined so fast that it is off the monitoring scale. The cuckoo was once the signature sound of the British summer up until about a decade ago, but today it is a rare experience to hear its distinctive resonating through the woodland foliage.

Bambi, I'm sorry to report, is one of the main suspects and is currently under investigation. (Unfortunately, he's exercising his right to silence, which is delaying the inquiry.) Most species of deer, notably the little muntjac, have been increasing over the same period that the birds have been disappearing. Deer live in the woods too, and it is thought that their constant foraging and prancing about through the undergrowth is damaging nesting sites. Another cause, at least in part, is the disappearance of the shrub layer, caused by changes in woodland management and the decline in traditional coppicing.

The main problem, however, may turn out to lie thousands of miles away in sub-Saharan Africa where the evidence is growing that all is not well for our migrant birds. Four of the five woodland birds showing the steepest drop are summer visitors while eight out of ten of the species suffering the greatest decline of all British birds are long-distance migrants. This suggests that either the birds are encountering difficulties on their journey to and from Africa, or that their habitat there has been gravely compromised by environmental degradation and the clearance of forests for agriculture.

British birds showing major increases in recent years

Wood pigeon	Carrion crow
Collared dove	Greenfinch
Magpie	Goldfinch
Red kite	Raven
Greater spotted woodpecker	Sparrowhawk
Pheasant	
Swallow	
Blackcap	
Great tit	
Nuthatch	
Jackdaw	

The wholesale slaughter of the albatross

For centuries, an albatross following a ship has been seen as a good omen. It was believed that the birds carried the souls of dead sailors, watching over the ship and crew. If there is any truth in the sailors' superstition that to kill or injure an albatross brings bad luck, then the crews of the world's long-line fishing fleets are in for some serious ill fortune.

British naturalist Sir David Attenborough is just one of many high-profile public figures who have added their voices to the increasingly urgent campaign to save the albatross from impending disaster. "Albatrosses have survived in the harshest marine environments for 50 million years; more than 100 times longer than our own species," he said recently. "However, these magnificent birds are unable to cope with man-made threats, such as long-line fishing."

Nineteen of the world's 22 albatross species, as well as storm petrels and shearwaters, are seriously threatened by "long-lining," a form of intensive fishing where lines measuring up to 80 miles long are fitted with thousands and thousands of baited hooks. The lines are pulled through the oceans, many of them by pirate fishing crews, in search of highly lucrative catches such as tuna, swordfish and Patagonian toothfish that will fetch hundreds of thousands of dollars.

Seeing flocks of other birds feeding off the discarded fish waste and bait from a commercial fishing boat, the albatrosses are drawn to these death-traps like bees to a honey pot. The baited lines, thrown overboard by the fishermen, float for a few fatal minutes before sinking beneath the waves. The albatross, an expert at feeding off the water's surface, swoops to take the bait. Immediately the large hook rips into the throat and as the line starts to sink the choking albatross is dragged under to a hideous death.

Once they have reached maturity (between 7 and 12 years), most species of albatross will breed every other year as it takes the better part of 12 months to incubate the one egg and raise the chick. When an albatross fails to return to the family nest, the chick will die. Left to themselves, the birds live for 60 years but they are currently being killed in such huge numbers that they can't breed fast enough to keep up with the rate of their extermination. Conservative estimates put the annual death toll at 100,000, meaning one albatross dies every five minutes. While you are reading this, one of the world's oldest and most majestic birds will be having its throat torn out by a giant hook.

Simple ways for fishermen to halt the slaughter of the albatross

- Use colorful plastic streamers suspended over the long lines at the back of the boat to scare birds away from baited hooks.
- Use underwater chutes to let out the long lines.
- Use blue-dyed bait to make it hard for the birds to see it.
- Lay fishing lines at night.
- Add weights to fishing lines so the baited hooks sink faster.

In addition to these practical steps the commercial fishing enterprises can take themselves, government action is needed to stamp out pirate fishing.

Undefended coastline

Conservation groups are furious that the British government will not bestow greater protection on marine wildlife sites that are home to 18 species of fish, mammal, bird or reptile considered at risk of global extinction. They point out the glaring discrepancy between the treatment of marine and inland sites – all the more frustrating given that only three such endangered species depend on land or fresh-water habitats. The UK's coastline hosts huge populations of waterbirds that are reckoned to be the country's greatest contribution to global biodiversity. The great skua, Manx shearwater, gannet and shag have their most important populations in the world on Britain's coasts, while the puffin, kittiwake and guillemot also rely on British waters for breeding. In the future, campaigners insist, even greater demands will be placed upon an already highly fragile marine environment. Under European law, the UK has protected only three marine sites of importance to birds, fewer than tiny Latvia, even though the UK's coastline is 25 times longer.

REFERENCES

Addison, Joseph, *Spectator*.

Allen, Glover Morrill, "Birds and Their Attributes" from *The Bedside Book of Birds* by Graeme Gibson, Marshall Jones Company, 1925.

Beeton, Mrs., *Beeton's Book of Household Management*, Wordsworth, 2008.

Bewick, Thomas, *A History of British Birds,* 1816.

BirdLife International and the International Union for the Conservation of Nature.

Brontë, Anne, "Views of Life" from *The Complete Poems of Anne Brontë*, ed. Clement Shorter and Charles W. Hatfield, Kessinger Publishing, 2008.

Deval, Jacques, "Afin de vivre bel et bien."

Ellis, Havelock, *Impressions and Comments*, Houghton Mifflin, 1918.

Fisher, James, *Watching Birds*, Penguin, 1941.

Fisher, James and Lockley, Robert, *Sea Birds: An Introduction to the Natural History of the Sea-Birds of the North Atlantic*, Collins, 1954.

Freud, Clement, *Freud on Food*, 1978.

Genesis 8:6–12, New American Standard Bible, 1995.

Hudson, W. H., *British Birds*, 1895.

Jung, Carl, *Psychology and Religion*, Yale University Press, 1977.

Kington, Miles, *Nature Made Ridiculously Simple*, Penguin, 1983.

Langland, William, *Piers Plowman*, Penguin Books, 1959.

Lanier, Sidney, "The Owl Against the Robin" from *Poems*, ed. Mary D. Lanier, BiblioBazaar, 2007.

Lawrence, D. H., "Self-pity" from *The Complete Poems of D. H. Lawrence*, Wordsworth Editions Limited, 1994, reproduced by permission of Pollinger Limited and The Estate of Frieda Lawrence Ravagli.

Longfellow, Henry Wadsworth, *Evangeline: A Tale of Arcadie*, Biblio Bazaar, 2008.

Longfellow, Henry Wadsworth, *Hyperion: A Romance*, Dodo Press, 2008.

The Medieval Bestiary, http://bestiary.ca.

Merritt, Dixon Lanier, "The Pelican."

Nicholson, Max, *The Art of Birdwatching*, H. F. & G. Witherby, 1931.

Peattie, Donald Culross, *Singing in the Wilderness*, G. P. Putnam's Sons, 1935.

Pope, Alexander, "Windsor Forest" from *Selected Poetry: Alexander Pope*, Oxford University Press, 1998.

RSPB Big Garden Birdwatch, 2007.

Service, Robert, "Bird Watcher" from *Collected Poems of Robert Service*, Warner Books, 1993.

Thomson, James, *The Seasons*, 1805.

Thoreau, Henry David, *Walden, or Life in the Woods*, Dover Publications, 1995.

Wesley, John, *Journal*, 1790.

Whitman, Walt, "The Dalliance of Eagles" from *Leaves of Grass*, Everyman, 1993.

Wordsworth, William, "The Recluse – Book First" from *Home at Grasmere*, Penguin Books, 1986.

Wordsworth, William, "The Solitary Reaper" from *William Wordsworth: Selected Poetry*, Oxford University Press, 1998.

Young, Roland, *Not For Children*, Garden City Publishing, 1945.

ACKNOWLEDGMENTS

It takes a small army of people to produce a book like this. Editors, copy-editors, illustrators, designers and proofreaders, backed up by squadrons of assistants, all play a crucial part in ensuring the book is fit to go to the printers. It has been my good fortune that my publishers have a superbly professional team to pave my way and clear up the mess I leave in my wake. So thanks in particular to Susanna Wadeson and then, in alphabetical order, to Deborah Adams, Hugh Adams, Lucy Davey, Elizabeth Dobson, Geraldine Ellison, Manpreet Grewal, Phil Lord, Richard Shailer and Katrina Whone. Thanks as always to Araminta Whitley at literary agents Lucas Alexander Whitley (LAW) and to my friend Steve Apps for his patience in pointing out and describing all the different species living within binocular range of my home. I reserve most of my gratitude, however, for my sister-in-law Olivia Pemberton who inspired me to write the book. Without her curiosity and enthusiasm, the project would never have taken wing.

INDEX